NURTURING WELLNESS
through
RADICAL SELF-CARE

NURTURING WELLNESS

through

RADICAL SELF-CARE

A Living in Balance Guide and Workbook

JANET GALLAGHER NESTOR

LICENSED PROFESSIONAL COUNSELOR
DIPLOMAT IN ENERGY PSYCHOLOGY

BALBOA.
PRESS

A DIVISION OF HAY HOUSE

Balboa Press books may be ordered through booksellers or by contacting:

Balboa Press
A Division of Hay House
1663 Liberty Drive
Bloomington, IN 47403
www.balboapress.com
1-(877) 407-4847

Because of the dynamic nature of the Internet, any web addresses or links contained in this book may have changed since publication and may no longer be valid. The views expressed in this work are solely those of the author and do not necessarily reflect the views of the publisher, and the publisher hereby disclaims any responsibility for them.

The author of this book does not dispense medical advice or prescribe the use of any technique as a form of treatment for physical, emotional, or medical problems without the advice of a physician, either directly or indirectly. The intent of the author is only to offer information of a general nature to help you in your quest for emotional and spiritual well-being. In the event you use any of the information in this book for yourself, which is your constitutional right, the author and the publisher assume no responsibility for your actions.

Certain stock imagery © Thinkstock.
Any people depicted in stock imagery provided by Thinkstock are models, and such images are being used for illustrative purposes only.

ISBN: 978-1-4525-6051-9 (e)
ISBN: 978-1-4525-6050-2 (sc)

Library of Congress Control Number: 2012920830

Editor: Deanna A. Stephens

Printed in the United States of America

Balboa Press rev. date: 11/26/2012

Heartfelt thanks to:

Helene Cestone, for your editorial help with the initial manuscript; Stephanie Nestor for your wise insight and editorial support; Jennifer Nestor-Cardwell, for the photo session that produced my photo for this book; Phil Warren, for sharing your wisdom so freely and for the initial invitation to be part of the in-office development team for REB; my husband, for his love and his support of my work and writing; my friends, who listened and commented wisely during the writing of this book; and Kirtan Coan, thank you for the great photographs, some of which ended up in the book. To the original volunteer Nurturing Wellness group members: Without you this book would not exist.

Nurturing Wellness through Radical Self-Care is dedicated to Stephanie and Jennifer, my beautiful daughters. You are the light of my life, the rainbow in my sky, and a love that inspires me to be the best that I can be.

CONTENTS

. . . .

PART 1. NURTURING WELLNESS THROUGH RADICAL SELF-CARE GUIDE

CHAPTER 1

CHAPTER 2

CHAPTER 3

PART 2. NURTURING WELLNESS THROUGH RADICAL SELF-CARE WORKBOOK

PART 3. REB SELF-CARE FOR LIFE

PART 4. RESOURCES AND REFERENCES

FOREWORD

When Janet asked "The Shift Doctors" to write the foreword to her book, *Nurturing Wellness Through Radical Self-Care,* we were delighted. As an Integrative Psychiatrist (Dr. Latz) and a Transpersonal Psychologist (Dr. Ross) who are both trained metaphysicians, energy medicine practitioners, and holistic/qigong healers, we both have written books, recorded DVDs, mindfulness and guided meditation CDs, and taught personal transformation courses about holistic approaches to wellness and shifting personal as well as global consciousness. In addition, Dr. Latz has written numerous articles on trauma and post-traumatic stress disorder. Our passion and purpose of giving rapid, easy-to-use tools to assist people who are ready to get out of maladaptive reactive patterns, transform negative thoughts and baser emotions (anger, guilt, shame, abandonment, fear, heartache, inadequacy, etc.), and to 'Shift Your Life' seemed to be a natural fit to Janet's approach.

Humans are naturally wired at birth for joy and playfulness. It is our natural state until we learn not to be in it. Just observe a young child before they have become socialized or worried about performing, disappointing, etc. They are happy and carefree. As we experience life's hurts, disappointments or traumas, we can become entrenched in a state of fear, or "fight or flight or freeze." Our adrenal glands can go into overdrive to keep us in an anxious, fearful state; we can become fatigued with lack of purpose or awareness of who we truly are.

Janet's book gives tools and a program for both patients and therapists to assist with stopping the fight-or-flight response. It can allow a person who has been living in a fearful state to become more peaceful and centered, to hold space to begin to "wake up" and learn to create differently in their relationships, their body, and their life.

When we reconnect with our natural neurological state of joy and happiness we can weave the fabric of our lives from our heart center, employing joy, love, compassion, wisdom, and intuition. We can walk our paths from a proactive rather than reactive state of being. We are expressing our resilience, vitality, and joy. We allow ourselves to BE in the NOW.

Traditional Chinese medicine, which is one of the oldest forms of healing documented on the planet, describes a flow of energy called the 'strange flows' or 'Radiant Circuits'. These subtle energies respond immediately when needed by a meridian or other energy system that is in deficit. These flows respond to all of our thoughts and emotions as they connect and harmonize our energy systems. The importance of activating and energizing these circuits regularly to produce inner joy and the 'physician within' cannot be underestimated.

We believe in the concept of Janet's book and workbook because we know it works! We (and many of our colleagues) have had enormous success in using energy medicine tools and techniques with patients in psychiatric and counseling practices as well as in our own Shift Your Life seminars. We have taught for the past several years about Radiant Circuits that naturally produce joyfulness and were quoted in SELF magazine in the article "Wake Up Happier," (November 2008) where they found (much to their surprise) that use of 'figure eights' was the only one of four techniques that gave EVERY person an inner sense of well-being to some degree. We are thrilled that Janet is bringing Radiant Circuits and their benefits to the attention of more therapists and to those seeking self-empowerment.

Unfortunately most of us are rarely in this state of joyful consciousness. In our hectic daily lives we create stress as our thoughts race from the previous task to the next on the list, the traffic, what we have left undone, and then we often react from negative patterns which have nothing to do with the current events and circumstances in our lives. This can lead to our suffering ill health from tight muscles, colds, back ailments, obesity, migraines, auto immune diseases, and other physical issues to psychological symptoms like depression and anxiety, among other things. Our ideal state is lost and we become victims of unhealthy choices we didn't know we could avoid.

The four principal building blocks of Janet's program, Radiant Energies Balance (REB), mindfulness, affirmations, and journaling, can be easily incorporated into a daily dharma or practice to assist in stopping the mind chatter, and feelings of overwhelm, and creating inner peace, or centering. This is a starting point to begin to address shifting faulty thoughts to re-pattern thinking and empowering people to be able to make different choices for their lives coming from the circumstances of the present moment. These tools allow you to quiet the mind to prepare you to begin the journey to access your intuition and connect with your inner wisdom, and they empower you to develop to your highest potential in mind, body, and spirit.

Enjoy Janet's book—it just might Shift Your Life! Janet Nestor is a woman of great heart, compassion, and inner wisdom. Allow her to share some of it with you in the pages of this guide and workbook.

Wishing you well and Bright Blessings on your inner journey,
Tracy Latz, MD, MS, and Marion Ross, PhD, MhD
(a.k.a. "The Shift Doctors" at www.shiftyourlife.com)
Authors of *Shift: 12 Keys to Shift Your Life*

PART 1

NURTURING WELLNESS

through

RADICAL SELF-CARE

GUIDE

CHAPTER 1

Living in Balance

Balance is the key to a long and happy life.

If you are too happy or too excited, happiness becomes exhausting.
If you are too sad, your light dims, your world darkens.

If you love too much, you lose yourself.
If you love too little, you never find yourself.

If your day is too long and too full, you are overwhelmed and burnt out.
If your nights are filled with fear and worry, you are unable to sleep.

If you work too much, you are overwhelmed and exhausted.
If you work too little, you become a victim to yourself.

If you are hungry and the pantry is bare, all you can think about is food and your hunger.
If your table is laden with food, your hunger is satiated; your mind is full of other things.

If you are eager for knowledge, there are not enough books to quench your desire.
If you are content with your knowledge, you can't find a book worth reading.

If your life is unorganized and without priority, balance is lost.
If life has purpose and order, balance presents itself without effort.

When your life is chaotic, balance and harmony are impossible.
When balance is in your life, harmony is always within reach.

In balance, you are love.
In love, you are balanced.

~ *Janet Gallagher Nestor*

Introduction: Choosing Wellness and Well-Being

What motivated me to develop the Nurturing Wellness Through Radical Self-Care Program? The answer is easy. I know how wonderful it is to feel empowered, and I know how deeply you want to feel better than you do today. This statement is true whether you are burnt out and exhausted, or you are moving through life with relative ease, hoping to find more meaning and joy.

As a mental health professional, I believe that all addictions behave relatively the same; and I believe that fear, anxiety, and worry are often successfully treated similar to addictions because they separate us from life in the same way that substance addictions (food, alcohol, drugs) and behavioral addictions (gambling, sex, pornography) separate us from life. They numb us out, keep us in denial, prevent us from facing our life issues, or temporarily and manipulatively protect us from overwhelming emotional–spiritual pain. While Dr. Katie Evans believes that anxiety disorders and addictions are two different illnesses, she brilliantly compares them on a chart in her Hazelden Co-Occurring Disorders Series pamphlet called "Understanding Major Anxiety Disorders and Addiction" (2003, 5–7). When you look at the causes, symptoms, and recovery programs, they are strikingly similar. You can also read *Losing Pounds of Pain* (1994) for Dr. Doreen Virtue's insights about the role of chronic stress in the development of eating disorders.

"Nurturing Wellness Through Radical Self-Care" suggests that you create a new habit of daily energetic self-care. Energetic self-care means realizing and accepting that Earth is an energetic planet and you are an energetic being who needs to replenish your energy just like your car needs a refill of gasoline. The skills taught in this book give you an opportunity to combine Radiant Energies Balance (REB) with meditation, journaling, and affirmations. You'll learn to use a new Energy Healing exercise that is easy, quick and effective, helping you establish and maintain a balanced chakra system, providing more efficient energetic nourishment for your entire mind–body system.

Radiant Energies Balance is a unique meridian-based energy psychology because it simultaneously creates relaxation and release of negative emotional blocks. It encourages inner balance. Many of the energy psychologies use affirmations, or positively stated intentions, to strengthen their ability to unearth the deepest levels of an issue, providing relief. Mindfulness teaches now-centered living developed through the adoption of conscious awareness and positive thought. Journaling helps put us in touch with our deepest feelings and our intuition. Together, these four approaches help you create positive new habits, change negative beliefs to positive beliefs, reduce inner tension, overcome emotional road blocks, and build a highly functional relaxation response. You and I can't be healthy if our autonomic nervous system (ANS) is out of balance and our relaxation response is broken. The more out of balance our ANS becomes, the greater likelihood of chronic illness. This is a book about creating a balanced autonomic nervous system and an efficient, working rest–digest response. I hope you'll find it useful both personally and professionally. It is highly effective for the majority of people.

At one time I was a teacher for educationally and emotionally challenged adolescents who were tired of the fight to achieve. Many were exhausted and experienced little hope of academic or social success. Most wrestled with high anxiety, fear of failure, low self-worth, and poor self-efficacy. My job was to teach, but before my students could learn, the environment had to be calm, positive, compassionate, accepting, and designed to provide both encouragement and structure. All academic direction had to be properly sequenced, organized, and clearly stated to insure a positive flow of easily digested information. My handouts had to enhance each student's ability to integrate the information while simultaneously strengthening their ability to use the content in action-oriented ways. The same educationally sound guidelines were applied when planning and writing this program for you. It is user-friendly, self-empowering, positive, and leaves you in charge of the pace and the content of your individual program.

Some, maybe even many, who choose the Nurturing Wellness Through Radical Self-Care Program are emotionally and physically exhausted because of chronic anxiety and worry. Some have trouble focusing because of long-term stress, and others are fearful that this program is just another technique that won't work. Some of you are trying to keep your head above water as you agonize about a loved one with an eating disorder, addiction, illness, or other life-threatening condition. Some of you have a handicapped family member: a child, a spouse, a sibling, a parent. Some of you are trapped in a bad marriage or have family history that continues to rule your life. Because you want success that is obtained in a natural setting and in a natural way, this program is designed to provide instant hope to guide you steadily toward positive personal transformation. The daily **Nurturing Wellness Journal** and **Self-Care First!** pages are self-exploratory in nature and give you a convenient place to record your progress and insights.

During childhood I learned to pretend to accept behaviors and ideas that caused me emotional pain. It was a hard habit to break. My loving, and simultaneously overprotective and neglectful family overflowed with addictions: cigarettes, alcohol, food, relationships, anxiety, and fear. As a three- and four-year-old I sat quietly beside my great-grandmother while she endured the terror of severe panic attacks. For years, I watched a ritualistic drama unfold each time the sky turned dark and cloudy. At the first sign of a thunderstorm my great-grandmother crossed the dirt road to my grandparent's house where I lived. My grandmother and her mother walked from window to window, closing the blinds to block out the lightning. All things electric were unplugged. Sometimes the electricity was turned off at the fuse box. My grandmother then went into her bedroom and kept the door closed while my great-grandmother pulled a strait-back chair into the corner of the kitchen and sat stoically with her hands folded in her lap until all signs of the storm were gone. I sat quietly across from her at the kitchen table. During the storm the house was a tomb. My orders, lovingly given, were to be quiet and sit still. I obeyed. Somehow, I grew up loving the sound of the rain pattering on the roof and windows—and unafraid of thunderstorms!

Even so, I had panic attacks as an adolescent and carried a lot of fear and anxiety into adulthood. Today, years after my childhood experiences and deep into my professional career, I continue my personal growth journey. Moving and resting meditation, breathing meditation, and self-hypnosis quiet my mind, keep me in touch with my deepest inner needs, and allow me to dance with the joy within. Energy Psychology, when used as prevention and release provides a quick and efficient way to work on day-to-day issues as well as a way to process the "big stuff" when it comes along. My goal is to live a fully conscious, mindful life.

The Nurturing Wellness Through Radical Self-Care Program was originally written for my clients with food issues and eating disorders. During the first trial group (2006) I realized there were far-reaching benefits for everyone. The second trial group (2007) included individuals with fibromyalgia, chronic fatigue, eating disorders, depression, chronic anxiety, panic disorder, grief, loss and trauma, and individuals from various 12-step recovery groups. Simply put, this program attracts people who want to feel healthier, happier, and more content with themselves and their lives.

I have an adolescent female client with the perfect genetics for attention deficit disorder, sensory integration disorder, learning disabilities, major depression, panic disorder, and disordered eating. She is tall, thin, beautiful, artistic, depressed, and anxious. Her mother feels so "guilty" about the family genetics that merged in just the right way to "give" her daughter this array of challenging symptoms. We all can relate to her guilt and feelings of helplessness. As parents, we want the best for our children. However, guilt is not a solution to any problem as it creates an imbalance within. We owe them a positive and nurturing environment, food, shelter, clothing, the appropriate medical treatment, and a good academic education, simply because we birthed them. As good people and parents we owe ourselves self-love, continued growth, and development toward positive relationships with ourselves, our children, our life partner, and any others we love and hold emotionally close to our hearts. When we seek the help and emotional support we need and are providing for our children in the best way we know how, we are doing our job as parents. We are meeting our personal responsibilities. We let our children down only when we live in denial, refusing to face our own issues or ignore theirs when they are struggling.

Why do you have the problems you have in your life? Why do our children face the stress and illnesses they suffer? Why do some of us grow up in a dysfunctional, chaotic family? Why are some people emotionally sensitive and easily overwhelmed? Why does one couple divorce and another with similar issues work it through? Why do some die of their illnesses while others live and thrive? These questions have no easily obtained answers, and the answers that do exist are very complex. Yet, life has an ultimate order and consistency. Your life is not an accident of birth, and we don't accidentally meet our teachers and helpers: they are provided for us. Each of us has built within us the wisdom of Creation and the knowledge and ability to heal emotionally, physically, and spiritually. We aren't born with instructions, so we have to search for and find our individual wellness, sense of well-being, and inner peacefulness.

Wellness is our hope and our goal. Living in balance is essential to achieve our goal. REB and the Nurturing Wellness Through Radical Self-Care Program can help you find and maintain your balance and your center of well-being.

The Philosophies of Nurturing Wellness Through Radical Self-Care

Healing

I have chosen to share a philosophy of healing that was defined for me a year or so ago during meditation. This new way of thinking is going to change your life and the lives of those you love and cherish. You'll change your self-talk and change the way you interact with members of your family when they are sick or suffering. It applies to the work you'll encounter during your Nurturing Wellness Through Radical Self-Care Program. You'll have some new things to consider as you choose your strategies for a positive life journey.

Every person alive is interested in the concepts of health and healing. Health determines the quality of our lives. The word "healing," the way we usually think of it (but not the way we use it) indicates a positive change taking place within our mind, body, emotions, and spirit—or within our family system. But, if we are not careful, the word "healing" can take on negative implications. I am asking you to raise your level of awareness.

Most of us feel we have to heal our emotional and physical wounds in order to achieve robust health. We feel that we have to draw upon outside resources in order to accomplish overall well-being. If we are sick or injured we are interested in our speed of healing, wanting to heal as quickly as possible. If we are anxious or depressed, we want those feelings to disappear. When asked how we feel about our illness or injury, we reply almost unconsciously using negative concepts that are deeply ingrained within our hearts and minds. Often our replies sound similar to these:

- "I'm healing. I've been impatient, but I am gradually getting better."
- "I never thought I'd still be healing from this illness after all these months. I'm ready to go back to work, but I'm not quite up to it."
- "I've had better days. I'm tired all the time, and I nap a lot."
- "Why did I have to get so sick? I'm tired of being in the house all the time and tired of being a burden to my family."

Each time we think or speak the word "healing" in this way, we indicate that we are somehow broken or impaired by events such as surgery, the flu, a car accident, an early life trauma, a fight with a family member, or the loss of a loved one. Think about the innocent words you and I might have spoken, completely unaware of their implications. Within the same sentence we've used the word "healing" in association with words like illness, suffering, and death to create what I refer to as a negative pairing. A negative pairing occurs when the word "healing" is placed with words related to a weakened state of being, disease, and suffering. Words like "illness" and "disease" are lower frequency words and perceived as negative, therefore carrying a negative emotional–physical impact. When we habitually pair a high-frequency, positive impact word like "healing" with low-frequency negative impact words, we inhibit our mental–physical–spiritual ability to heal.

Negative phrases such as, "this illness has been exhausting" reinforce the fact that your illness has lasted a long time and you've had to fight your way through it. "I am finally healing" might be said to mean, "I was so sick I thought I was going to die." Our carelessly spoken words actually reinforce our suffering and support our current perception of suffering. They remind us of our emotional–physical struggle with illness, feeding our mind and body negative messages about the ability to heal. Each time you innocently say words similar to those above, you may be slowing your recovery in any current and all subsequent illnesses by declaring, "I'm a slow healer" and "illness threatens me." The more positive we are, the more we pair positive words and concepts together. The more we pair positive words and concepts together, the healthier we become.

Healing is not about recovery from illness, surgery, or divorce. It is about our virtues, or the positive aspects of self: acceptance, wellness, joy, kindness, love, tenacity, vigor, tenderness, and compassion. When we embrace our virtues and incorporate their energy into our perception of life, we uncover our capacity for wholeness and wellness. Discovering and embracing our inner light, our potential, is the true spirit of healing. It is the realization of this empowered healing spirit, this limitless potential that I want to share with you.

> **Healing is achieved through:** Turning on the light of your soul and allowing it to shine. Living from your heart center and within the awareness of your own light. Living within high frequency virtues that support and sustain a positive, robust life. Trusting in the process of life and trusting your own wisdom. Filling your mind with positive thought. (See a full list of virtues on page 219.)

Here are some examples of how you might put your new definition and philosophy of healing into use. Rather than say "I am finally healing from the flu," it is much better to say "My body is strong and getting stronger every day." Instead of saying "The worst is behind me now, and I continue to heal from my injury," it is more positive to say "My body is a miracle and very good at its job." By changing the way you express yourself, you begin to use positive words to define your healing and recovery. You'll learn to do this as you use this program to unleash your internal power and your inner peacefulness.

Energy Psychology

Energy Psychology is a group of comprehensive, brief, and powerful mind–body mental health therapies that came into being in the mid-1980s. The first energy psychology,

Thought Field Therapy (TFT), was developed by psychologist Roger Callahan, PhD. It led to the development of many methods you read about today, Gary Craig's Emotional Freedom Technique (EFT) being the most widely known and used. Radiant Energies Balance (REB), the technique we use in this book, is categorized as an energy psychology because it is a meridian-based method of relaxation and emotional release that is similar to TFT and EFT. Other energy psychologies like Advanced Integrative Therapy (AIT), developed by Asha Clinton, use the chakra system to help you obtain and maintain health and well-being. Let me share briefly about the importance of balanced meridian energy, the energy system we use with Radiant Energies Balance.

Your meridians flow energy (chi) through enclosed channels within your body. Each meridian channel has several acupoints, the same ones used in acupuncture, that when stimulated, encourage the body toward inner balance. The 12 strategically located meridians flow chi either from crown to foot or from foot to crown. They energetically feed each of your major organs: heart, lungs, kidneys, liver, large intestines, small intestines, spleen, pancreas, urinary bladder, pericardium, and gall bladder. The Central Vessel, the Governing Vessel, the Triple Warmer, and the Spleen/Pancreas are individual meridians that also work together as the Radiant Circuits. The Central Vessel regulates the six yin (feminine, more passive) meridians: Spleen, Kidney, Liver, Gall Bladder, Bladder, and Stomach. The Governing Vessel regulates the six yang (male, more aggressive) meridians: Lung, Heart, Pericardium, Triple Warmer, Small Intestine, and Large Intestine. In Chinese Medicine philosophy, yin-yang balance is seen as important in maintaining good health and overall well-being.

REB is perfect for our use because it is a relaxation therapy, a release therapy, and an autonomic nervous system (ANS) balance. This means that while you are relaxing at a meditative level you are subtly balancing your ANS and letting go of stress, worry, life issues, and the various emotions that have been stuffed down and bottled up for years. You'll learn more about the benefits of REB as you work toward building your cued **relaxation response,** which naturally occurs when you use the REB posture.

Relaxation Response: "a deep state of rest that changes the emotional and physical response to stress, and is the opposite of the flight or fight response."
Dr. Herbert Benson, MD, Harvard School of Medicine

National and international organizations have developed to enhance and support the growing new field of Energy Psychology. Three of the most well-known Energy Psychology organizations are in the United States, the United Kingdom, and Canada. These three organizations offer training and certification programs, and they have established ethical standards for certified practitioners.

The Association of Comprehensive Energy Psychology (ACEP)
www.energypsych.org
233 East Lancaster Ave, Suite 104
Ardmore, PA 19003
ACEP was co-founded by Dorothea Hover-Kramer and David Gruder in 1999.

The Association of Meridian and Energy Therapies (The AMT)
http://theamt.com
45 Gildredge Road Eastbourne
East Sussex BN21 4RY
United Kingdom
The AMT was established by Dr. Silvia Hartman and Chrissie Hardisty in 1998.

Canadian Association for Integrative and Energy Therapies (CAIET)
www.caiet.org
414-221-5639
Ontario, Canada
CAIET was founded in 2008 by Dr. Sharon Cass Toole, PhD, CCA, DCEP.

Mindfulness

Mindfulness has become popular in the United States as Mindfulness-Based Stress Reduction (MBSR). MBSR education began in 1979, developed by Dr. Jon Kabat-Zinn, PhD, at the University of Massachusetts Medical Center (www.umassmed.edu/cfm/stress/index.aspx). Mindfulness refers to a calm and peaceful approach to life and has the ultimate goal of creating a mindfulness lifestyle, meaning a relaxed intellectually, emotionally, spiritually aware way of life. MBSR combines mindfulness and yoga, both flowing from Eastern healing and spiritual philosophies. Mindfulness and yoga concentrate on breathing and the creation of inner alignment and fitness. In our work, we'll combine mindfulness, energy psychology, journaling, and the use of affirmations. I believe this combination of approaches is an exceptional way to create inner harmony and the integration of mind, body, spirit, and emotion. The incorporation and regular use of our Radiant Circuits, also known as the circuits of joy, helps harmonize every system within your body, establishing and maintaining your relaxation response, creating a sense of well-being and inner peacefulness.

During the REB Nurturing Wellness Through Radical Self-Care Program, we work to achieve "a mindful lifestyle." A mindful lifestyle is defined by the following ideals:

- Conscious connection to *self* and *creation*
- Conscious decision-making with clear awareness
- Living a now-focused life

- Living in gratitude
- Understanding the mutuality of all life
- Living in harmony with each other and the world around us
- Positive self-worth and good self-confidence
- A feeling of self-love and connection with life, others and the all living things

The main ingredient of a mindful lifestyle is positive thought. Positive, mindful thought is based in the principles of unconditional love and is achieved when:

- Each thought has a positive intention
- Each thought has positive content
- Each thought produces a positive outcome for self, others, and for all life in general

Information adapted from Pathways to Wholeness *by Janet Gallagher Nestor (2010).*

Every word we think or speak is a type of energy and creates either a positive or negative frequency (charge) within and around us. As we mentioned earlier when we discussed the use of the word "healing," the frequencies we create with our words and thoughts affect our decisions, our relationships, our employment, our success, our failures, our health, and our wellness. Have you ever walked into a room and "felt" such strong negativity you wanted to turn around and run? Maybe you have approached someone at a social function to introduce yourself and felt a barrier that said very clearly you were not to approach them. Instead of extending your hand in greeting you merely said hello and turned your attention elsewhere. Have you walked into the home of a new friend and instantly felt welcomed, not only by their greeting, but by the cozy feeling and the positive energy that permeated every nook and corner of every room? These scenarios illustrate the diverse experience of coming into contact with a negative, low-frequency energetic situation and a positive, high-frequency situation. The difference is immediately recognized in our entire mind–body–spirit system.

Positive thoughts help us construct a positive life, one thought at a time. Most of us have thoughts that are not entirely positive. Some of us have some very negative beliefs about ourselves and about life. Neutral thoughts do not have a frequency strong enough to create a positive life.

Negative statement: "You know, I worry so much about everything."
Positive statement: "I am grateful for today and accept the challenges I'll encounter."

The word "worry" is both a word and a frequency. "Grateful" is both a word and a frequency. Worry has a very low-frequency vibration causing us to feel anxious, heavy, and depressed. Grateful is a high-frequency word causing positive emotional responses that lighten our mood. The initial heaviness created by the "worry" frequency creates concern, and suddenly we have established a negative thought chain. All the negativity we have created can carry us emotionally downhill at the speed of light. We are caught up in worry and begin to worry about the worry and the anxiety it creates. Unless we break our negative thought chain we stay caught up in it. Every day at least one person asks me "How do I stop worrying?" I usually say that there is a way out of worry addiction. And there is. It is my hope that the growth opportunities in this book will help you move out of worry and into a new freedom.

Moving out of a worry addiction is a "process" activity. Living and learning are "process" activities. A "process" activity is one that progresses in natural steps at a rate of speed that is comfortable for the person who is moving out of worry addiction, learning, or making other positive change. We learn step one, grasping its full implications. We move to step two, grasp the concept, understanding it, gaining the ability to apply it in our daily lives. Our natural growth process moves us forward as our wisdom and our ability to apply it expands. Our decision-making improves and our quality of life is richer and fuller. We notice we are happier and instead of being overwhelmed we are more positive and confident. Over time we acquire the awareness and the abilities needed to move to step three and on to step four.

We move ahead one step at a time, one day at a time: we live in process and understand that it is a natural, normal way to live. We accept that real and lasting growth takes time. *Nurturing Wellness Through Radical Self-Care* is a process workbook. For example, we progress from birth to preschool skills, to elementary school skills, on to middle and high school, and then to adult living skills. The natural life process does not take us from infancy directly to adulthood. We have to live the years between. It is interesting to know that personal growth is sometimes defined as living in process with grace and acceptance. Anne Wilson Schaef discusses the art of living in process in her book by the same name, *Living in Process* (1999). Wilson Schaef is one of the premier writers in the fields of addictions and co-dependency. Three of her notable books are: (1) *365 Mediations for People Who Worry Too Much;* (2) *Beyond Therapy, Beyond Science: A New Model for Healing the Whole Person;* and (3) *Co-Dependence: Misunderstood–Mistreated.*

When living in process, we gradually learn to live our best life. We all want to live within freedom, hope, and unconditional love, but we don't always know how to make that happen. The first step is to understand what it means to live within these great, high-frequency virtues. When we live within freedom, hope, and unconditional love, we strive to achieve the following environment within our personal life—especially within our family life. Ideally each family member will:

- think and act in positive ways
- honor the natural interdependence of family life
- allow independence within family togetherness
- live each day with a hopeful, joyous heart
- develop a positive sense of self, including worthiness
- experience a sense of belonging
- make loving, appropriate, reality-based decisions
- be accountable for their behavior
- ask for support when wanted and needed
- embrace peacefulness
- offer and receive respect
- feel safe
- trust
- enjoy emotional intimacy with family and friends
- enjoy emotional intimacy within our romantic relationship
- feel compassion for dysfunctional family members, current and past
- believe in our personal power and ability to write our own life story
- live within our healthy belief system
- have fun and laugh a lot
- live within a healthy life plan, one day at a time
- love deeply, wisely, with joy and passion

From Pathways to Wholeness *by Janet Gallagher Nestor (2010).*

During the 90-day Nurturing Wellness Through Radical Self-Care Program you'll use a mindful **Nurturing Wellness Journal Page** to record your experiences when working with Mindful Meditation, REB, and the Nurturing Wellness Affirmations. You'll be tracking your moods and jotting down a daily gratitude that helps you create a positive outlook for your day. You'll be using the **Self-Care First!** page to help you plan and participate in activities that give you much-needed social contact and positive, effective exercise. Exercise does not mean you have to take up jogging or go to the gym every day. Exercise can mean walking up and down the stairs two times in a row, going for a meditative walk each day, or doing some deep breathing and stretching. If bedridden, it can mean imagining yourself going for a walk and enjoying nature. There is some research-based evidence indicating that to imagine yourself exercising and moving around freely has positive psychological and physical benefits. See Dr. Andrew Weil's website for an easy to read explanation of the obtainable physiological benefits of guided imagery. http://www.drweil.com/drw/u/ART00468/Guided-Imagery-Therapy-Dr-Weil.html

Each Nurturing Wellness Through Radical Self-Care group session that I lead begins with a mindful meditation and closes with each person stating a positive intention for the week ahead. Since you'll be doing the Nurturing Wellness Relaxation and Release work, you'll want to stay in balance by self-recording or listening to the mindful meditations that are included in this guidebook then writing about them in your mindfulness meditation journal. You can find them recorded for you at www.mindfulpathways.com.

Affirmations

"Effective affirmation is 20 percent what you know and 80 percent what you feel about what you know." ~Jim Rohn

Affirmations are statements of positive intention and can be used daily to stimulate positive change in our lives. They are examples of positive thinking on steroids! The benefits are both conscious and unconscious. Affirmations, when coupled with REB, become much more than a positive statement. The REB posture connects you with four meridians: Spleen, Triple Warmer, Central, and Governing Vessels, that do double-duty as Radiant Circuits. The Radiant Circuits, also known as the Circuits of Joy, are intelligent hyperlinks that engage when needed, providing feelings of overall well-being. (*Energy Medicine,* 1999: Donna Eden) When you engage the REB posture and speak an affirmation, you stimulate balance within your whole body. You also engage the Radiant Circuits which naturally work to provide you with a sense of joy and well-being. The following is a brief explanation of the four meridians that serve as Radiant Circuits. Seeing the difference between balanced and unbalanced can help you visualize the transitions you are making using this program.

Spleen Meridian: Balanced—Fairness and Compassion Toward Self
Unbalanced—Overly Compassionate and Worried About Others

Triple Warmer: Balanced—Feelings of Safety
Unbalanced—Engaged when Danger is Perceived, Fight-or-Flight Response

Central Vessel: Balanced—Feeling Centered and Secure
Unbalanced—Feeling Vulnerable

Governing Vessel: Balanced—Sense of Inner Strength
Unbalanced—Lack of Courage

Meridian Information from *Energy Psychology Interactive,* 2004:
David Feinstein, PhD; ww.rebprotocol.net: Phillip Warren with Janet Nestor

Here is the science of how affirmations work: Familiar thoughts carve a pathway in your brain, making it easier to think that same thought again. Each time you repeat the same affirmation, it makes the neurological pathways stronger. "Neurons that fire together, wire together" is a good little rhyme that illustrates what happens. Neural synapses that are seldom or never used get efficiently eliminated by the brain. Neurons that are routinely fired in a specific pattern strengthen their bond, "wiring together" a network that will automatically fire whenever triggered by your thoughts. If you are wiring positive thoughts together, your neurons fire when a similar positive thought or incident occurs. If you are wiring together negative thoughts, your neurons fire when a related negative thought or incident occurs. Why not think positive and build positive neuropathways that serve your overall well-being? If you are having trouble following the neuropathway explanation here is a good analogy about creating a path through the woods. As you walk the route the first time, you tramp down the grass. Eventually the grass begins to wear away and because you keep walking in the same place, it does not grow back. Finally you have a packed down dirt path with no grass at all, one that is easy to trek. You made the path, one walk at a time, over many weeks of traveling the same route (Maddie Ruud, http://maddieruud.hubpages.com/hub/Self-Affirmations).

Your experience with affirmations might not be very positive. I know that I thought them almost useless for many years because I was not using them wisely. There is some research that tells us that affirmations can actually create inner conflict for the person using them. This is true when an individual tries to make themselves repeat an affirmation they absolutely 100% don't believe or one they are opposed to for some reason. I talk about this later in the book, but now is a good time to introduce this concept so when you begin your work with our affirmation lists, you will do so in a wise and productive manner. I'll use the idea of "living in process" to explain how to use affirmations successfully.

A person who has just committed adultery and lost their marriage is going to find it hard to say, "I love and respect myself just the way I am." At the moment they loathe themselves, but they do want to grow into the positive self-affirming statement. The emotional jump from self-loathing to self-love is just too big for them. Healing the self-loathing is a "process" that might begin gently with self-compassion. They'll need to re-write the affirmation above to reflect their place along the healing process. Their first-step affirmation might be "I am compassionate with myself just the way I am today."

If you're reading and learning in order to begin your Nurturing Wellness journey, this might be the affirmation for you: "I am open and willing to work the Nurturing Wellness Program."

Journaling

Keeping a journal is a magnificent way to manage stress and anxiety, create change, develop positive thoughts and beliefs, and get in touch with unconscious wants and needs.

Journaling is a perfect complement to mindfulness, energy psychology, and affirmations, which reinforce each other and support you with great power.

The Nurturing Wellness Journal page, part of the Nurturing Wellness Through Radical Self-Care workbook, is more of a log than a classic journal (see page 109). It helps you track your moods and get in touch with feelings that occur as you work the program. Most of all, it is a great way to keep track of your program choices and monitor your progress. **This Week's Insights** page (see page 107) gives you a place to jot down ideas, comments, and questions that come up—and you will definitely have them. Everyone who has worked with this program has needed more room to write their comments, insights, and ideas. Writing is the best way to bring ideas and insights into reality and teach yourself how to apply them to your life. I am always going through my journal looking for something I've written because it applies to an insight or idea that came up today.

You'll also be keeping a **Mindfulness Meditation Journal.** You can either purchase a notebook for your journal or create a folder on your computer to record your responses. You'll love and appreciate this journal! After each meditation, you are asked to write about the feelings, insights, and thoughts you experience during your meditation. You will *want* to take the time to do this. And believe me, as one who meditates and then journals immediately afterward, the journal is priceless. Of course there are days when I have little to say, but on other days I have volumes of feelings and thoughts I want to remember and apply to my life. Re-reading my meditation journal is like reliving my meditative life. It is inspiring. Sometimes I am amazed at my own insights and I wonder why some idea or thought didn't make a greater impact. Reading it again allows me to embrace the insight more fully and apply it in a way that might have been unavailable to me earlier.

The **Self-Care First!** page (see page 108) is both a tracking journal and an activities log. It is meant to encourage gentle exercise and other self-care activities that support the development of your relaxation response along with the re-balancing of your ANS. Sometimes when we are busy, preoccupied, or sick and tired of being "sick-and-tired," we just want to kick back, watch television, and think of nothing. Although television or videos might be temporarily distracting, even relaxing, they don't have the ability to balance your autonomic nervous system or improve your physical or emotional health.

Suggestions for Success

Each person engaged in *this* growth program is going to find success. Each person defines his or her own success and builds it gradually. One small change couples with a new belief and suddenly you realize you are making progress. If you are part of a group, please don't compare yourself to any of your group members. Comparisons are negative thought processes and don't work for anyone. What others might be doing or accomplishing is irrelevant to your growth as you progress through your program.

If you are "just exhausted" and "at your wits' end" (in fight-or-flight mode) prior to beginning this program, substitute Mindful Meditation, Mindful Meditation with Radiant Energies Balance, and Breathe, Imagine, Relax for the Readiness Affirmations. These meditations, especially Mindful Meditation with Radiant Energies Balance, "cool" down your autonomic nervous system and give you deep relaxation and heightened awareness.

Your key to success in all things is balance. During the 90 days of the Nurturing Wellness program, plan some "fun stuff" every week. Take days away from the program and focus on something other than personal growth. Get a massage or schedule an energy-healing session with a Healing Touch or Reiki practitioner. Take some nice, meditative walks. Laugh whenever you get an opportunity, and if there isn't an opportunity, make one. Go to a ridiculous movie and laugh out loud. Go out to dinner with your goofiest, funniest friend and have a great time. Laugh! Enjoy life.

It is very hard to have fun when you are overwhelmed and exhausted because a loved one is suffering from a serious or life-threatening issue. This kind of exhaustion is both emotional and physical, and it demands that you replenish yourself daily. Fear and worry are debilitating emotions and caregivers need a lot of tender love and care, from themselves, family members, and friends. Caregivers often over-do until they are absolutely worn out. If you are a caregiver and you haven't reached total exhaustion, this is your opportunity to avoid that pitfall. This program will not only support your health, but help you grow your self-compassion and feelings of self-worth. It will help you find your joy even when you think you'll never feel joyful again. It will help you learn to approach both adversity and joy with a balanced response. Living your life in balance is well worth any effort it takes to create an equilibrium that is right for you.

For those of you who have developed a chronic physical or emotional health problem, this program supports your journey into a much higher state of wellness and well-being. The Nurturing Wellness program provides a method of deep and compassionate self-care. You are guided to stay in the moment, maintain a positive approach to life, develop self-love and self-worth, to play and have fun, and incorporate some meaningful exercise into your daily life. Even if you are unable to get out of bed, you can participate in this program. A mindfulness lifestyle coupled with your use of the REB posture supports your immune system, your emotional health and well-being, and helps you develop the ability to relax deeply any time you have a few moments to spare. You can use the posture during medical treatments (explained in greater detail on page 210 if the REB posture does not interfere with the mechanics of the treatment. You can use the posture while listening to music or TV, even though TV interferes with the deepness of the relaxation experience. It is flexible and easy, and you can use it anytime and anyplace without fear of embarrassment or criticism. No one will even know you are relaxing and balancing your autonomic nervous system.

Balance is built into the program and it is up to you to accept the balance that is suggested. Addicts and individuals with anxiety often feel that more is better. During this program, and in most life situations, more is not better. Forced work only postpones your growth process. A balanced approach enhances the benefits of the program and everything about you, on every level of your being.

CHAPTER 2

Adrenal Fatigue and Your Autonomic Nervous System (ANS)

Knowing the effects of autonomic nervous system (ANS) imbalance is essential to health and well-being. Stress is a constant in most everyone's lives, yet we know little about where most of our stress comes from and know even less about how to eliminate it. Too many sleepless nights and too much worry create imbalances throughout our whole mind–body–spirit system, and there are many unrecognized stressors that burden it. Awareness is the first key to achieving an overall sense of well-being. Knowing the origin of our stress is a step in the right direction. You can find parenting stress indexes and job stress indexes that are very insightful. The very informative "Total Stress Load Index" created by Dr. CE Gant, MD, PhD, (http://cegant.com) is outlined below so we can all begin to learn about various sources of stress and maintain total mind–body health and well-being.

12 Stressors and the Total Stress Load Index (TSLI)

1. Emotional Stress (e.g., losses, post-traumatic)
2. Cognitive Stress (e.g., irrational demands)
3. Sensory Stress (e.g., chronic pain disorders)
4. Metabolic Stress (e.g., low/high blood sugar)
5. Toxic Stress (e.g., heavy metals, chlorine)
6. Immune Stress (e.g. autoimmune, allergy)
7. Infectious Stress (e.g. Lyme, Candida, GI)
8. Purposelessness Stress (e.g. no spirituality)
9. Endocrine Stress (e.g. hormonal, PMS, aging)
10. Oxidative Stress (e.g. vein/arterial blockage)
11. Energetic Stress (e.g. electromagnetic, geopathic)
12. Neurotransmitter Stress (e.g. low or high levels)

About Stressors and Their Effects on the Body

There is no such thing as isolated stress. The impact of stress is always system-wide. For example, if you break your arm, your body goes into action: you feel immediate pain (sensory stress) signifying something is wrong, your adrenal glands (hormonal stress) begin to produce stress hormones, and you experience increased heart rate and faster breathing. If help is not readily available there is a good chance you'll experience emotional (trauma response) and cognitive stress (irrational thinking) states that may increase your physical pain.

Organs and Glands Affected by Chronic Stress

Brain, muscles, pancreas, thyroid glands, adrenal glands, stomach, intestines, liver, kidneys, bladder, genitals, lungs, eyes, heart, sweat glands, salivary glands, digestive glands

Psychological and Physical Effects of Chronic Stress

Fear, guilt, sadness, anger, willfulness, aggressiveness, irritability, depression, burn-out, emotional depletion, hopelessness, insomnia, infections with slow healing rate, chronic illness

Partial List of Dis-ease and Diseases Associated with ANS Imbalance

- Adrenal Fatigue
- Depression
- Anxiety Disorders including Severe Panic Attacks
- Thyroid Disease
- High and Low Blood Pressure
- Breathing and Swallowing Problems
- Erectile Dysfunction in Men
- Chronic autoimmune diseases: (e.g. Lupus, Chronic Fatigue, Fibromyalgia, Celiac Disease)

If you find the information above interesting, you can easily learn more about the effects of chronic stress by reading the reliable information at the following websites:

1. National Institutes of Health:
   www.nlm.nih.gov/medlineplus/autonomicnervoussystemdisorders.html
2. The Merck Manual Online:
   http://www.merckmanuals.com/home/brain_spinal_cord_and_nerve_disorders/autonomic_nervous-_system_disorders/overview_of_the_autonomic_nervous_system.html

Naming Our Symptoms

Prolonged stress causes the human body to make adaptations so it can continue to serve you at a functional level. The more stress, the more adaptations. The adaptations often cause serious illness in the forms of adrenal fatigue and autonomic nervous system imbalance. If there isn't an intervention, adrenal failure occurs. Adrenal fatigue isn't considered an official diagnosis by many physicians, yet it has become known as hypoadrenia. Severe adrenal failure is called Addison's Disease and is recognized by modern medicine (*Adrenal Fatigue*, James L. Wilson 2011). The dysregulation of the autonomic nervous system does have an official name: Dysautonomia. Dysautonomia brings with it a group of illnesses that affect many areas of the body. Dr. CE Gant calls Dysautonomia "the primary cause of all physical and psychiatric disorders." (http://cegant.com)

The following are examples of Dysautonomia-related illness.

Pure Autonomic Failure (Idiopathic Orthostatic Hypotension)

Orthostatic Hypotension is a degenerative disease of the ANS

Symptoms:

- Dizziness
- Fainting
- Weakness and Tiredness
- Visual Disturbances
- Cognitive Disturbances
- Tremors
- Vertigo
- Pallor
- Anxiety
- Tachycardia (heart palpitations)
- Nausea
- Neck Pain
- Chest Pain
- Fatigue
- Sexual Dysfunction
- In advanced states the patient is bedridden or wheelchair bound, can stand less than 1 minute
- Occurs later in life and women are affected less often than men

("Idiopathic Orthostatic Hypotension and other Autonomic Failure Syndromes," Dr. Mohini Gurme, MD, http://emedicine.medscape.com/article/1154266-overview. *Clinical Autonomic Disorders 3rd Edition*, Phillip A. Low and Eduardo E. Benarroch 2008.)

Autonomic Neuropathy (damage to autonomic nerves)

- Caused by alcoholism, abnormal protein build-up, autoimmune diseases like Lupus, Rheumatoid Arthritis, some cancers, diabetes, damage from some medications, Parkinson's Disease, HIV/AIDS

(Autonomic Neuropathy Definition: staff, www.mayoclinic.com/health/Autonomic Neuropathy/DS00544. *Clinical Autonomic Disorders 3rd Edition*, Phillip A. Low and Eduardo E. Benarroch 2008.)

Familial Dysautonomia (FD)

- Genetic autonomic condition, particularly effects Ashkenazi Jews
- Early infancy onset and exhibits in failure to thrive, poor ability to suck (nurse), unexplained fever, blotching of the skin
- Sensory system disturbances and ANS dysfunction

(Dysautonomia Foundation, INC (FD), www.familialdysautonomia.org. *Clinical Autonomic Disorders 3rd Edition*, Phillip A. Low and Eduardo E. Benarroch 2008.)

An exceptional, easily understood site for more information: "It's Dysautonomia, Not Laziness," http://clinicalposters.com/news/2011/0325-dysautonomia-mitochondria-pots.html (ClinicalPosters.com staff).

Making Changes: Information to Help You Reduce Your Total Stress Load

We have warning signs that let us know when we are sick. The primary tip-off that our adrenal system is failing is frequent illness with longer than normal recovery time (*Adrenal Fatigue,* James L. Wilson 2011). As we discussed a little earlier, our autonomic nervous system becomes imbalanced for many reasons because we exist on many levels of being. Our physical body is affected by our environment including all the places we visit, vacation, study, work, and worship within, the level of allergens and toxins we come in contact with, our foods and the chemicals they are treated with during their growth and production, our spiritual health … the list goes on and on. James L. Wilson (*Adrenal Fatigue,* 2011) and Dr. Joseph Mercola (www.mercola.com) each created a list of things to be aware of when your autonomic nervous system is overworked and you are experiencing adrenal fatigue. The items on the list below can create chronic stress within the body, but often go undetected. We can get so used to a stress that it feels normal to us. When the stress is relieved, we are amazed at the relief we experience.

Evaluate Dr. Mercola's list below to determine the areas where you can create positive changes in your health and well-being.

- watches, beepers, cell phones (EMF Reduction)
- food allergies
- psychological / emotional issues
- spiritual issues / conflict
- dehydration
- nutritional deficits / too many fast foods
- heavy metal exposure / toxicity
- frequent respiratory infections and other infections that are undiagnosed
- geographic fields
- electromagnetic interference
- malocclusion (poor tooth alignment)
- structural problems
- scars
- energetic imbalances within your body's organs
- solvents, pesticides, herbicides
- man-made prostheses
- visual issues

James L. Wilson gives us a list of lifestyle components that can lead to adrenal fatigue and autonomic nervous system imbalance (*Adrenal Fatigue,* 2011). This list helps raise our awareness:

- lack of sleep and staying up late even when fatigued
- poor food choices and using food and drinks as stimulants when over worked or overtired
- living or working in situations that create feelings of powerlessness
- constantly driving yourself or feeling rushed
- the need for perfection
- living or working in no-win situations (double binds)
- the lack of enjoyable and rejuvenating life activities

There are some stressful situations that are relatively easy to remediate, are free or nearly free, and relieve a great deal of stress within your mind–body–spirit system for overall improved health. The first and the easiest is *hydration*. Make sure you are drinking plenty of good, clean, fresh water. We don't think of water as being "alive," but fresh water found at its source is energized and vital. Processing changes the PH and the electrical charge of water and makes it less beneficial to our body. Natural spring water or well water has not been chemically altered with purifiers and fluoride, circulated through a public water treatment plant or piped into your home. Just like fresh fruits and vegetables that are raw and viable, clean water that's closest to its original state is better for you.

Secondly, it is fairly easy to monitor your *food intake* and increase the amount of nutritional, organic foods in your diet. I try to buy organic in the grocery store and purchase fresh food from a farmer's market as often as possible. I usually have a small garden in the summer so I have a few fresh veggies I can pick. Even if you live in a city apartment, you can have a window garden or find a place for a few pots on a tiny balcony.

There are inexpensive, natural ways to test and *treat allergies.* One of the most widely known was developed by Sandi Radomski, ND, LCSW (Licensed Clinical Social Worker) and is called Allergy Antidotes. Stemming from the work of Dr. Roger Callahan's Thought Field Therapy, Allergy Antidotes accomplishes success through: (1) Assessing whether substance sensitivity is the cause of the presenting issues; (2) Identifying specific reactive substances; and (3) Using Energy Psychology Techniques to reprogram the body to no longer react negatively to the substance. An Allergy Antidotes practitioner list is found at Sandi's website, www.allergyantidotes.com.

The second widely known natural method, and the oldest, is called NAET or Nambudripad's Allergy Elimination Technique founded by Dr. Nambudripad, a chiropractor, acupuncturist, kinesiologist, and registered nurse. It is a combination of energy balancing and treatment techniques from acupuncture / acupressure, allopathy (Western medicine), chiropractic medicine, nutritional medicine, and the field of kinesiology. One reactive substance is treated at a time and if your immune system is strong, you may need only one treatment per reactive substance. NAET is available all over the world and you can find a practitioner at www.naet.com.

When anxiety is high and is disrupting your life, it is good to *eliminate several foods*. Among the most challenging to your body are: sugar products; caffeinated coffee; caffeinated teas; chocolate, because of caffeine and sugar; caffeinated sodas, especially diet sodas; and anything with artificial sweetening, especially aspartame. Cigarette smoking is a terrible source of stimulants and chemicals, and ultimately it heightens your anxiety and panic. In her book *Living Well with Chronic Fatigue Syndrome and Fibromyalgia* (2004), Mary J. Shomon recommends the incorporation of good fats like olives, avocados, fish, nuts, and seeds into your diet. She also advises correcting nutritional deficiencies with good-quality, easily digestible nutrients—organic when possible.

Next, consider the *importance of the human energy system*. Without a functioning energy system your body can't exist. Our body systems run on electrical currents (chi, life force energy) that flow through our meridians and spin within and from our chakras. Because of these facts it is necessary to learn as much as we can about electromagnetic fields (EMFs) and their impact on our health. While the dangers of EMFs are still controversial, there is enough evidence that some medical professionals are making their patients aware of the possible negative effects. Sometimes it is possible to avoid high EMF areas by simply exploring a neighborhood prior to moving into a new home or apartment. If the home you are interested in is near a power station, a cell phone tower, electrical lines, and transformers, you might want to reconsider moving there to avoid a higher level of EMF exposure. This is true especially if you have young children.

If you are extremely sensitive and concerned, you might want to purchase a gaussmeter, an instrument that measures the EMFs in your home. One of the easiest things you can do is walk around the outside of your home to locate the main electrical power source. In some homes everything electrical enters the house in one general area: phone lines, TV cable, the power companies meter and wiring, air conditioning units. If the room next to the power source for your home happens to be a bedroom, move the bed as far away from the connections as possible. If you have an electric clock beside your bed, move it across the room. Go to the store and purchase electrical outlet protectors that many of us use when our children are small. Place them in all the empty outlets around your home, especially the ones in your bed room. Use your speaker phone when talking on your cell phone or another device that keeps it as far from your body as possible (*Adrenal Fatigue*, James L. Wilson 2011).

We all have a scar somewhere on our body, and we really don't view it as a medical problem. Scars, especially scars that are raised and hard, can cause energy flow issues within your body. I had a surgical scar that my holistic physician felt was causing abdominal complications. After a few treatments with bio-puncture (acupuncture with homeopathic remedies) the scar softened and became less of a problem to energy flow, allowing my abdomen to be energetically fed. Surgeries cut through meridians and chakras. As an energy practitioner, I recommend that everyone be energetically balanced prior to surgery or a medical procedure and have an energetic treatment for re-balancing as soon as possible after the intervention. Radiant Energies Balance (discussed on pages 12, 56) is an excellent way to prepare for surgery along with many other energy healing modalities. Most energy healers will tell you that energy work speeds healing and prevents many negative side effects after invasive medical treatment. When I was working primarily as a Reiki teacher and healer, I noticed that women, post-breast cancer surgery, complained of large numb areas on their arms and sometimes their chest. These numb areas are due to lymph removal and the surgical incisions. Their doctors told them the numb areas were something they'd have to live with for the rest of their lives. Fortunately that was not true. For most women the numbness left completely. For others, only a small nickel or quarter sized area remained numb after several Reiki sessions. Even abdominal numbness, often occurring after repeated abdominal surgery, can be lessened or eliminated with energy healing work.

If you are constantly tired, worn out and always getting sick, or often have flu-like symptoms, there is a possibility that you have chronic fatigue, fibromyalgia, or both. There is substantial evidence that these illnesses are caused by microorganisms that are not typically identified in our usual lab tests. You can ask for a special lab test called PCR (polymerase chain reaction tests), which detects the microorganisms that are causal in these particular illnesses (*Adrenal Fatigue,* James L. Wilson 2011).

There are many alternative healing systems and modalities that support the development of a balanced autonomic nervous system and adrenal health. The following styles of medicine can be helpful: Osteopathic (DO), Traditional Chinese Medicine (TCM), Naturopathic (ND), Ayurvedic (DAy) and Chiropractic (DC), Board Certified Holistic MDs. The following energy bodywork methods alleviate stress and normalize the body's energy system:

- Healing Touch
- Reiki
- Body Talk
- Energy Psychology
- Jaffe-Mellor Technique (JMT)
- Physical Therapy and all the various types of massage are very effective because they help with pain, stress reduction, and help promote good energy

flow. Physical therapy helps to preserve mobility and increase physical fitness (*Living Well with Chronic Fatigue Syndrome and Fibromyalgia,* Mary Shomon 2004. *Chronic Fatigue, Fibromyalgia and Lyme disease, 2nd edition,* Burton Goldberg and Larry Trivieri, Jr. 2004).

CHAPTER 3

Mindful Meditation Defined

For me, mindful meditation is peaceful communication between self and Creation—a quiet inner focus, directed toward silencing my mind. It is the unification of the mind–body–spirit systems responsible for creating well-being and the awareness of inner knowing. Rob Nairn, a South African Buddhist teacher and author, defines it as "... a highly alert and skillful state of mind because it requires one to remain psychologically present 'with' whatever happens in and around one without adding to or subtracting from it in any way (www.psychologytoday.com/articles/200105/the-science-meditation). Master T.T. Liang, author of *T'ai Chi Ch'uan for Health and Self-Defense,* says of Tai Chi or moving meditation "you are in a trance; your five attributes (form, perception, consciousness, action, and knowledge) are all empty—this is meditation in action and action is meditation," (*T'ai Chi Ch'uan For Health and Self-Defense,* 1977).

However you define mindful meditation, it changes the way your brain functions, and the positive change in brain function changes the way you live your life, your degree of contentment with life, and your sense of personal joy. It is your friend. Allow it to introduce you to yourself, maybe for the first time.

Breathing in, I calm my body.
Breathing out, I smile.
Dwelling in the present moment
I know this is a wonderful moment.

~ Thich Nhat Hanh

Learning to Appreciate the Little Things

I know that some of you are challenged by the idea of meditation. During the Nurturing Wellness Through Radical Self-Care Program, we'll approach meditation from a non-critical, non-judgmental point of view and hold the belief that your ability to meditate will improve as your autonomic nervous system begins to balance and you become more compassionate and loving toward yourself. You are asked to appreciate who you are right at this moment, with all your good qualities right along with all the things you want to change.

Some of you have learned to stop feeling in order to survive. This means that you live your life each day with all of your pain buried deep within your body, mind, and spirit. Others of you have been so overwhelmed by your feelings that they are all you can think about: you don't have time to think about the good things that are going on in your life. Now all of a sudden, you are asked to be alert, to be consciously aware of your thoughts and feelings and how you experience them. You are asked to notice the tension and the areas of your body that express the stress. You are asked to create positive change within your heart, your mind, your body, your emotions, your spirit, and your energy field. You are asked to become aware of the tiniest things that you would normally overlook or slough off as irrelevant. The tiniest bit of progress is as important as sudden, noticeable change. A tiny change here and a bit of a change there will accumulate, eventually adding up to a big, noticeable, positive, life-altering change.

Almost anyone can be flooded by emotion during meditation. Most of the time the emotions are wonderful and loving, creating a state of emotional bliss. Occasionally there is a sudden release of stored-up emotion—an outburst of stored-up, stuffed-down feelings and thoughts. I always tell the story of meditating in my back yard on a nice, warm day in the mid-1980s. I was reclining on a lounge chair, letting the sun warm me and practicing a new meditation. I was in a blissful state, deeply involved. All of a sudden I was flooded with red hot scalding anger. I was stomping around my back yard wondering where in the world all that anger had been hiding and how it could be living inside me without my knowledge? I'd just been so quiet and peaceful! Yet, the anger and rage had been bottled up deep within me, out of my conscious awareness. The relaxation set it free so I could heal. It raised my awareness, and I took a step toward a higher level of well-being.

I'd never been told that I could release emotion like that during meditation. I want you to know that profound release of strong positive or negative emotion is possible. If this does happen, understand it is happening because you have successfully released enough pain to accept reality, heal, and feel again. To work through your experience, begin to breathe nice, slow, deep breaths. On the next *out* breath, allow the breath to drop into your lower abdomen. Continue to breathe from your abdomen for a little while. Allow your emotions to calm. Then, pick up your journal and write about your experience and the emotions that are now a part of your conscious awareness. Celebrate. Because of your continued work and your healing journey, there will come a day when you have no hidden emotions to release!

Most of our healing occurs during quiet moments of rest when we are in contact with unconscious feelings and experiences. I can't imagine life without the peaceful, insightful, educational moments I have during meditation. You will have moments when sweet calm moves through your body to soothe your mind, body, and soul.

Embrace your meditation experience, whatever it is. If you tear up, it is OK. If your mind continues to chatter, it is OK. If you spend time thinking how much you love your children, it is OK. If you barely notice any relaxation, it is OK. If you had to stop and go to the bathroom, it is OK. Accept your experience for what it is, accept yourself as you are at the moment, and make the commitment to keep meditating. The benefits are real, wonderful, life-affirming, and life-changing. All your experiences are important. Keep your thoughts positive, and you will continue to make progress.

The Nurturing Wellness Through Radical Self-Care Mindful Meditations

Meditation is another way to balance your autonomic nervous system, another way to stay emotionally and spiritually balanced, another way of getting fully acquainted with who you really are, another way to live in harmony with life. Mindfulness is intended to allow you and I to honor the very real connection between what we think and how we feel emotionally, spiritually, and physically. The approach is positive and self-affirming. Once you have learned the REB Relaxation Process, you can opt to combine this meditation with the REB posture, and you'll love the results. The REB Relaxation process teaches you to be in the moment, to be aware of what you are experiencing without being critical or controlling of the experience. The process takes you outside of your suffering as you learn to become a witness rather than emotionally attached and involved with every worry, ache, or pain.

Some of you may find you have the ability to reach a deep level of relaxation with your first meditation. Others will not. Most of us will find that sometimes it is easy to meditate deeply and other days are more challenging. We all have a learning curve and sometimes that curve winds around many obstacles before it is possible to become comfortable with meditation. Success comes from acceptance, so accept that mediation may take practice. Everyone is different, with unique life experiences, life issues, and genetics. Some of you have chronic anxiety or chronic depression. Others of you are ADD/ADHD. Some are distracted by chronic physical pain. Some suffer with autoimmune diseases like chronic fatigue syndrome and fibromyalgia. No matter what your personal or family problems are, quiet time and meditation provide the soothing moments necessary for wellness. Let the benefits multiply at their own pace, and remember to be grateful for the gifts you receive each time you are quiet and still. If you think quiet and stillness are impossible for you, think again. You'll gradually learn that you *can* achieve this rejuvenating state of being. Simply sitting quietly in the REB posture begins to balance your autonomic nervous system, and with that balance comes the ability to enjoy resting meditation and many other things.

During Mindful Meditation, place your mindfulness journal beside you with a pen or pencil. Once the meditation is over, immediately jot down any information you have gathered, any wisdom you want to remember, or anything you've learned about your mind, body, or spirit. During meditation you move out of conscious memory and the conscious workings of the mind–body into our unconscious memory and information that is almost always out of our reach during waking daily activity. Because you are in an altered state and using unconscious memory, you may not remember the information for more than a few moments after you are fully conscious and aware. Writing down your experiences accomplishes two things: It preserves the experience and assists your growth by helping you integrate the newly found information, information that usually resides in your unconscious mind, making it usable in your daily life.

You can relax with this meditation over and over again. If you choose, record the meditation in your own voice, or go to the Pathways to Wholeness Blog (www.mindfulpathways.com) and listen to the provided recording.

The Script for Mindful Meditation

As you prepare for your Mindful Mediation, make sure you have your mindfulness journal and a pen or pencil close to you. You'll want them for journaling once you've enjoyed your mediation.

Sit comfortably with your feet up or recline in a way that allows your energy to flow freely. Make sure that your neck and spine are comfortably aligned. If you are using a pillow, choose one that is thin and comfortable.

You can choose to close your eyes for the meditation or leave them open. I like to close my eyes because it improves my focus. If you choose to leave your eyes open, maintain a soft focus. In a soft focus, your eyes are at neutral, focusing on nothing in particular. It is almost as if you are staring out a window and seeing nothing except a smooth body of water or the expanse of a wide open valley clear of all obstructions.

Allow yourself to settle into a comfortable posture, feeling as though you are settling into your body. Notice your breathing and feel your spine. Imagine that you can feel your breath traveling up your spine with your *in* breath, and down your spine with your *out* breath. Inhale, beginning at the bottom of your tail bone, and up your spine to the spot where your head and neck join, and into the center of your brain where you visualize a little, translucent white pearl. Then bring your *in* breath to your brow chakra, on your forehead right above and between your eyebrows. On the exhale reverse the pattern, taking the exhale from the brow chakra back to the translucent white pearl, to the spot where your neck and head join, and down your spine to the bottom of your tailbone.

Feel your spine elongate and open. Using your imagination, see your spine open up and the energy begin to flow freely. As this occurs you may notice a color associated with your spinal energy. Some of you will see a bright, clear electric blue color, which is the energy of your nervous system. You can feel the relaxation flow into your face and your head. Your scalp relaxes. Your eyes, ears, nose, and mouth relax. Perhaps you feel a gentle smile on your lips and that further deepens the relaxation.

Begin to notice your body. Your shoulders are aligned, level, and relaxed. With each breath your shoulders become softer and increasingly more comfortable. The muscles in your arms become softer and looser as they relax. You notice your hands and fingers as they relax, and they feel alive and warm as energy flows through them.

Notice your hips. Your hips are aligned and level. As you notice them and the muscles soften, they feel more infused with energy and more relaxed. With each breath your hips and pelvic area become softer, more relaxed. As you inhale and exhale, feel your hip muscles continue to open, soften and relax. The relaxation flows down your legs, to your knees, your ankles, and into your feet and toes. You might find you want to wiggle your toes, flex your feet, or rotate your ankles. Move around in whichever way feels natural and positive. As your tension eases, you are more comfortable and at peace.

Imagine your bones, your skeletal system, automatically settling into the right posture to achieve the most comforting relaxation. As your bones settle into perfect alignment you notice an increased energy flow through your whole body. The correction increases the flow of energy to specific locations in your body, and you can feel the positive change taking place. You are soothed, and you continue to relax. The energy flows through each bone and your whole skeletal system feels aligned and harmonious.

As your skeletal system settles into perfect position for relaxation, you naturally and comfortably become more peaceful. Your body feels as smooth as silk—even, peaceful, everything flowing perfectly. You can feel the energy of love flow through you, through each bone, and your whole skeletal system. The increased energy enhances the communication between your mental self … your thoughts … and each bone in your body and between each bone in your skeletal system. It also increases the unconscious communications, enhancing your mind–body functioning.

Begin to notice the muscles and tissue that cover your bones and the nerves that supply energy to them—your whole neuromuscular system. You actually feel the muscles and flesh covering your bones. As your awareness increases, your senses provide information—there is communication between you, your bones, your muscles and the flesh that covers them and the nerves that feed them. You are comfortable in your awareness. You are interested in what information your neuromuscular system and your somatic sensory system provide about what is taking place within your body. Notice that your mind gently and completely accepts the comfort. Your body relaxes more deeply as your heightened awareness tells you it is OK to do so. You are completely at ease with the communication and the relaxation.

You notice that even though you are relaxed, you are also alert and highly attuned to my words. You are listening to the direction, and you are hearing every word clearly and interpreting the meaning in a deeply profound way. A sense of calm is settling over your entire body, and you can clearly follow each word that is spoken. Your awareness and insight is heightened.

You are using your *in* and *out* breath as your meditation focal point, and your breathing is naturally deep and regular. Your breath is the focal point for the meditation, and that is really all you notice—breathing in and out, soft and gentle. Your breathing is full and extremely comfortable. Your breath is soft and silken as it flows in and out.

Your breath flows comfortably as you inhale and exhale. If you notice a thought come into your mind, gently allow your mind to move away from the thought. Notice it. Honor it. Name it. Allow the thought to flow away from you on the next *out* breath. Your entire focus is on the breath and your quiet inner awareness. Your breath is naturally full. Breathing is automatic, natural, and comfortable.

Notice that each *in* and *out* breath is allowing you to drift gently into a quieter place—in and out—deeper into a relaxation that is soft, comfortable, and peaceful. You are content and comfortable in the pleasure of your relaxation.

With each breath you honor your whole self. With each breath you allow your mind to become more calm and restful. If a thought comes, notice it and let it move on. You have no attachment to the thought. Thoughts come and go. You are at peace. Your mind is quiet and still. You are grateful for your ability to relax in such a comfortable, peaceful way.

Breathe gently and normally—relaxing … noticing the completeness and deepness of the relaxation. The relaxation pleases you, is comfortable for you … is peaceful and restorative for you.

Each time you breathe, your relaxation is softer and deeper. With each breath you begin to have a greater awareness of who you really are; each time you meditate you discover something new about yourself, something new about your life. A new truth is always appearing, and that truth pleases you. Breathing and relaxing deeply is a lovely journey—a journey to self, a journey to your quiet space within, a journey to your own inner wisdom.

Your quietness and deep relaxation is helping your mind, body, emotions, and spirit integrate—communicate. The quietness is allowing you to center and balance your mind so your mind and body are functioning as a unit. There is a sense of wholeness, a sense that all parts are working together. Your breath is a soft, free-flowing ribbon of silk that balances your mind and body, creating unity within.

Listen quietly to what your mind and body whisper to you: What does your mind want from you? What does your body want from you? What does your mind–body system want from you? What does your mind–body system need in order to become more unified, to function at an increasingly more balanced level? Listen: focus on your breathing—

listening to your body ... fully experiencing your breath ... listening to your inner voice. You are breathing *in* and *out,* noticing your breath, listening to your body.

Experience your breath as it flows softly *in* and *out.* The experience is satisfying, deeply peaceful, and relaxing. Listen to your inner voice as it whispers its wisdom. You are calm and very still, and fully aware of your experience.

Allow your attention to move fully and gently into the compassion and love that exist within your heart. Focus on the love and compassion that is within your heart. Breathe love and compassion *in* and *out,* listening to your heart as it whispers quietly to you. Notice the gentleness of your heart energy, the love that is there for you. Notice the compassion that is there for you—and there for others. Notice the kindness and the joy that is part of your heart center. The kindness and joy are for you. Let your awareness of the heart center and heart energy grow ... as the energy of your heart grows, as the love, kindness, and compassion grow, allow your self-knowledge to grow with your heart's expansion— breathing *in* and *out,* following your breath, focusing on your heart center ... and your awareness of your gentle, loving heart center ... as it grows and expands.

Gently and softly, notice the love and compassion you have for yourself. Notice how comfortable it is for you to love you. Notice how comfortable is for you to feel compassion for you. With each breath, allow the compassion you have for yourself to expand and grow. Let the self-love grow until you feel nothing but love for yourself ... following our breath, breathing *in* and *out*—experiencing self-compassion and self-love. The self-compassion and the self-love are like a warm glow deep within. You may even be able to see the warm glow as it emanates from your heart center and flows into your whole being and on into your energy field until you are glowing from head to toe—and completely encircled by the glow.

Allow yourself to fully experience the softness and gentleness of the breath within you. Allow the softness and gentleness to move lovingly through your whole being—restoring ... rejuvenating. Each breath rejuvenates your whole being ... and you welcome the feelings of restoration and rejuvenation. You are aware of your own presence of being, and the awareness is magnificent.

Rest now. Rest deeply and fully. Rest in the quiet you have created within. Rest in the gentleness you are experiencing ... rest in the unconditional compassion you have for yourself—fully receptive to the love, receptive to the compassion. You are relaxed and enjoying the gentle compassion you feel deep within. You are smiling from within. The sun is shining on the inside and you are experiencing your own wholeness—your own unity.

Notice your breathing—the softness of your breathing—and once again begin to focus on your body, your whole being. As you notice your whole being, your entirety, your wise inner nature—there are messages there for you. Quietly give permission for your wholeness—your entirety—to share its deepest wisdom.

Breathing softly *in* and *out,* resting on your breath … relaxing with your breath … allow your breath to cradle you—to rock you gently in its loving embrace. Let your gentle *in* and *out* breath love you and care for you. The rocking is comforting … healing.

You are resting in your experience—quietly resting in your experience … chatting with your body … chatting with your inner wisdom. Allow the information to flow—whatever you want and need—resting and gaining awareness … soothing, gentle awareness … unconditional love of self—unconditional compassion given to you, by you.

(Transition to a more alert and aware state of consciousness.)

Gently and slowly begin to notice your body in a more alert way. Maybe you can feel your body as it reclines. Maybe you can feel your body awaken. Maybe you want to move your head or wiggle your hands and feet a little bit as you become more alert.

Continue to notice the love—the gentleness of the meditation process—the wisdom of the process. Notice your gentle, regular, effortless breathing and how it soothes you and cocoons you.

Gradually come fully present to the room, becoming more alert and clear. Come fully awake—feeling relaxed and refreshed … wiser … consciously noticing your increased awareness.

Once you are fully present, go to your mindfulness journal and write about your experience. The wisdom you record becomes a tool for your life. You can review the journal and your personal insights whenever you are led to do so. You are recording your truth, and your truth will continue to nurture and strengthen you.

Mindful Meditation with Radiant Energies Balance (REB)

Rest enhances healing; therefore, deep rest is essential for good health. When combined with Radiant Energies Balance, meditation allows you to rest and rejuvenate at a level many people can't obtain using meditation alone. As your mind rests, your emotions are soothed, internal communication is enhanced. As your autonomic nervous system becomes more stable and balanced, you are able to flow from stressful negative states to comfortable relaxed states with increasingly more ease and comfort. Imagine becoming aware of a challenging circumstance and being able to acknowledge it fully and rationally with acceptance. Imagine being able to recognize change is needed without becoming upset and agitated. Imagine being in a fender-bender and quickly being able to regain your composure, handling the situation with a clear, calm mind—and remaining calm after you get home!

Mindful Meditation with Radiant Energies Balance is a wonderful meditation to use when you are sick and tired of being "sick-and-tired." It is wonderful to use when you are at your wits' end. It is a self-given gift when you don't think you can handle tomorrow. It is wonderful on a sunny fall day when you have nothing to do but relax. It is wonderful any day you choose to use it.

The Script for Mindful Meditation with REB
<u>Desired Outcome</u>
A Desired Outcome is the result you want to obtain from your meditation. "Inner quiet" and "a feeling of connection" are two possible desired outcomes.

The diagrams below are here to give you a visual aide for the REB Posture and to help you with the directional hand movement for the heart massage. I suggest that you go to the end of the meditation and read the directions for the Heart Massage prior to listening to this mediation. REB is the central focus and the catalyst for deep, restful relaxation and the Heart Massage, a heart-centered energetic balancing activity, is used at the end of the meditation to help you integrate the positive feelings you obtained during your relaxation.

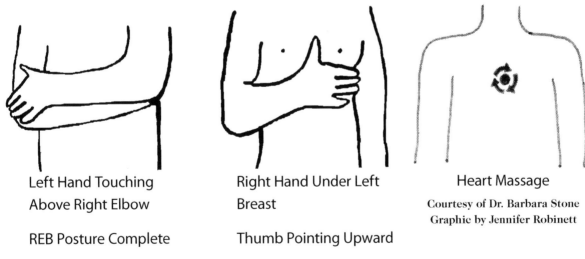

Left Hand Touching
Above Right Elbow

REB Posture Complete

Right Hand Under Left
Breast

Thumb Pointing Upward

Heart Massage

Courtesy of Dr. Barbara Stone
Graphic by Jennifer Robinett

www.rebprotocol.net

You'll want to journal when your meditation is over, so make sure you have your mindfulness journal and a pen or pencil close by.

Choose a time when you won't be interrupted. Sit or recline comfortably. Your head and neck and spine are aligned for positive energy flow and comfort. Allow your body to sink into its most comfortable position, adjusting your body as needed to create maximum comfort.

Take some nice, deep breaths and allow your body to begin to relax. Each breath takes you into a deeper state of soft and comfortable relaxation … to a place of love and emotional safety. Choose a desired outcome for the meditation … a virtue that you would like to embrace and experience more deeply in your daily life. Kindness, loyalty, love, comfort, freedom, creativity, joy, forgiveness, compassion, acceptance—choose the virtue that you want and need deep within. Keep your chosen virtue in mind and close to your heart as you drift deeper into the peacefulness you are feeling.

With your eyes closed, allow yourself to drift into a quiet, relaxed place—a deeper state of comfort and well-being. Begin to use the REB relaxation posture. Your right hand is resting on your body under your left breast with your fingers pointing under your arm, maybe they reach around to your side. Your left hand reaches across your body, resting on top of your right arm with the little finger of your left hand resting about an inch above your right elbow. Your ankles are comfortably crossed in the way that feels best to you. Your tongue is on the gum ridge behind your upper teeth. Your breathing is slow and easy with a nice, steady, even rhythm. As you rest in this posture you realize that you are more in the current moment, your mind is quiet, your thoughts have slowed and become less important to you. You can feel your nervous system calming and the inner tension lessening. There is nowhere you would rather be at this moment. Where you are feels soothing, safe and peaceful, comfortable and relaxing. You are exactly where you want to be—you are doing exactly what you want to do. You want to relax and rejuvenate. You welcome the feelings of relief and well-being you are experiencing. You cherish the calm, soft feelings that accompany the quietness you are creating within. You are peaceful and your thoughts are slowing … becoming quiet and still.

Begin to imagine that you can see yourself from head to toe as you breathe and relax. You can see your whole body as you hold the posture … and you have a conscious experience of your whole being. You notice what you are wearing. You notice how your body looks and feels as you relax. There might be a gentle smile on your lips and the image is soothing. The wholeness of the image is soothing and comforting to you. As you continue, breathe fully in a naturally deep way … each breath calming you … creating a feeling of wellness and well-being. Each breath transports you into a softer, deeper state of peacefulness.

As you relax within the feeling of wholeness, you begin to sense your own energy field. Your energy field surrounds your entire body and you can sense it. Perhaps you can see yourself within your energy field. It is as if you are floating in a highly energized bubble … floating right in the middle of the bubble. Your energy bubble is soothing and you feel surrounded by love. Notice that your energy field is both invigorating and soothing—full of life, full of vigor, yet calm and life-giving.

You are floating in your energy bubble and you are completely comfortable and deeply and peacefully relaxed. You see yourself as whole and you are experiencing a sense of wellness and well-being. You see yourself calm and relaxed, becoming safer, and more trusting. The longer you are aware of yourself within your energy bubble, the more relaxed and trusting you become. You are centered within the field. You feel balanced … connected to Earth, connected to life. You feel connected to Universal Love. There is a lot of love … and you are experiencing it as it flows through your entire being … warm, comforting unconditional love. Somehow you know beyond a shadow of a doubt that within this energy bubble, relaxed and calm, all good things are possible in your life. There are no limitations for your health and healing, no limitations to your emotional expansion, no limit to your experience of emotional freedom. You understand in a conscious, aware way what limitless actually means. You understand the full implications of your limitless potential. You feel loved and you feel safe. You are content and in touch with the wisdom within.

Bring to consciousness your desired outcome … the virtue you are bringing into reality. Focus on your desired outcome … the virtue you want to strengthen within your spirit. Begin to breathe in your desired outcome with each inhale, letting the energy of the virtue flow through your entire mind and body … touching every cell of your being … feeling the positive result as it flows through you. Breathe in this way, *in* and *out,* allowing your virtue to permeate each cell of your body, flow through your blood stream, touch your heart … quieting your mind. *In* and *out.* Absorb the virtue. Become the virtue.

(Pause a few seconds before continuing.)

You are now entering the closing phase of the meditation. You are beginning to become more aware of your surroundings and more aware of your body as it rests comfortably. You can sense the room around you and hear the sounds coming into the quietness. You continue to experience your body resting comfortably. You feel, and experience, total peacefulness, total calm, total mental quietness … your thoughts remaining quiet and still. The feeling of well-being continues to be with you and you notice all aspects of the well-being as you become more fully aware of your surroundings, more fully alert. The feelings of well-being, wholeness, and wellness remain with you.

When you are ready to do so, release the posture and complete a Heart Massage. Place your right hand over your heart, and begin to circle your right hand in a clockwise direction, moving your hand to the left and down and around and back up to the center of your chest. Repeat your chosen virtue over and over as you move your right hand in a clockwise direction. You might want to add a supporting affirmation that strengthens your experience.

When you are ready, open your eyes, feeling refreshed, calm, and clear.

When fully focused and present in the room, go to your special mindfulness journal and write about your experience. This helps you integrate your insights into all aspects of your daily life.

Guidance on how to complete a Heart Massage is repeated on page 67, in Chapter Four's discussion of additional release techniques (*Invisible Roots,* Dr. Barbara Stone 2008).

Breathe, Imagine, Relax Meditation

Breathe, Imagine, Relax is a unique meditation and a combination of Progressive Relaxation, Guided Imagery, Gap Breathing, and the healing energy of Laughter. Individuals who are challenged by a chattering mind find this meditation doable and very helpful. They soon learn their mind is quiet and still in the gap between their *in* and *out* breath and before the next *in* breath.

We carry stress in all areas of our body. We think about de-stressing tight muscles in our shoulders and our aching lower back, but often forget that stress and anxiety are universal, rather than localized to specific body parts. Progressive Relaxation, often called Progressive Muscle Relaxation (PMR), is one of the older relaxation techniques and has been around since the 1920s. It was developed by a physician, Dr. Edmund Jacobson, to teach us to relieve anxiety by releasing the tension in the muscles throughout our body. It is a very efficient means of relaxing and becomes even more so when combined with imagery and mindful breathing. Progressive Relaxation, as you'll experience it, is guided imagery that leads you through the various parts of your body, head to toe.

Progressive Relaxation, in its entirety, is featured in most stress reduction books and on many health and wellness websites (*The Relaxation & Stress Reduction Workbook*, Davis, Eshelman, and McKay 2008).

Guided Imagery is a very flexible therapeutic skill that supports your ability to stay balanced, centered, and fully present for life. It is based on the idea that your mind and body function together, unified to keep you healthy and happy. For example, if you are worrying and anxious, your body responds to the stress, goes into fight or flight, muscles become tense and tight, and mind–body is ready to spring into action, alert to perceived danger. If you feel safe and peaceful, your body reflects the peacefulness with soft, relaxed muscles and healthy, fluid mental–physical functioning. Relaxation, enhanced immune system, balanced autonomic nervous system and freedom from addictive behaviors are all possible benefits. You'll find that www.webmed.com is a good source of information about the practice of guided imagery. The website for the Academy of Guided Imagery, a well-respected education provider, can be found at http://acadgi.com.

I first learned Gap Breathing, a unique style of meditative breathing, in a Chi Healing class taught by a Tai Chi master. Gap Breathing teaches us there is a natural pause, or gap, after the *in* breath and again after the *out* breath—the pause offering a brief introduction to inner silence. It asks us to focus on the gap because the natural pause offers an amazing opportunity to get to know yourself, to gain wisdom about the miracle that is your body and the miracle of creation. In the gap there are no thoughts, and you are fully present for life and fully in your body. If you can experience that silence for a second, your inner knowing tells you that silence is always there for you and you can extend the amount of time you spend in natural quietness. Gap breathing is the ultimate mindfulness technique. I encourage you to explore Gap Breathing beyond this brief definition and your experience with Breathe, Imagine, Relax.

The old saying "laughter is the best medicine" introduced all of us to the idea that laughter is healing. A genuine smile and a good belly laugh, along with a good sense of humor, helps keep your body healthy and your thoughts positive. I speak about the power of the smile in my book *Pathways to Wholeness,* and laughter has been the topic of many books on health and well-being. You stir up the stagnant areas in your energy body when you laugh, and this causes positive change. You become more relaxed. Your thoughts are more peaceful. You feel happy and your stress magically disappears and does not return until your mind drifts back into old worry habits. In this mediation you give yourself a laughter break and reduce your stress through imagining laughter and then experiencing a full body laugh. An informative article, "Laughter is the Best Medicine," can be found at www.helpguide. org/life/humor_laughter_health.htm.

The Script for Breathe, Imagine, Relax Meditation
Remember to gather together your pen and mindfulness journal so you'll have it beside you as your meditation ends.

<u>General Directions</u>
Inhale from your abdomen. Hold the breath for a second. As you exhale, experience your whole self relaxing. Listen for the quietness in the gap between the inhale and exhale and again before your next *in* breath. There are miracles for you in the gap. This brief little meditation has created positive change for many people. It works for some people who find it challenging to quiet their racing thoughts.

Remember to pause and notice the gap after each segment. After the first segment, the directions become briefer. When you hear the word "pause" it is understood that you are to pause and notice the gap.

Take a nice, naturally deep breath, breathing from your lower abdomen … hold the inhale. As you exhale, relax your feet, ankles, toes, and the arches of your feet. Pause and notice the gap.

Breathe from your abdomen … hold the inhale briefly. As you exhale, relax your calves, knees, and thighs. Pause.

Breathe … hold … exhale … relax your pelvis, abdomen, stomach. Pause.

Breathe … hold … exhale … relax your chest. Pause.

Breathe … hold … exhale … relax your back, your spine, your lower back. Pause.

Breathe … hold … exhale … relax your shoulders, arms, hands, and fingers—allowing the stress and negativity to drain from your fingertips. Pause.

Breathe … hold … exhale … relax your neck, facial muscles, your scalp. Pause.

Breathe … hold … exhale … relax your eyes, ears, nose, mouth … add a gentle smile to your lips. Pause.

Breathe … hold … exhale and breathe fully and naturally from your abdomen. Pause.

Again, breathe … hold … exhale and breathe naturally and fully from your abdomen. Pause.

Breathe … hold … exhale … imagine a laugh massaging your internal body. Pause.

Breathe … hold … exhale … imagine a laugh rolling through your body, producing pure pleasure. Pause.

Breathe … hold … exhale … imagine that you hear yourself laughing with pure joy, and your body feels light and happy with the laughter. Pause.

Breathe … hold … exhale … laugh out loud. Pause.

As you complete the meditation—relaxed, clear, and focused—go to your mindfulness journal and write about your experience. Think about the natural pauses in your breathing. Explore your experience of the natural pause and the information available to you as you develop your ability to meditate.

Living in Balance: Harmony Mind–Body Energetic Exercise

The following energetic exercise is a perfect complement to the Nurturing Wellness meditations. It can easily be used as an alternative to Mindful Meditation and is in itself an exercise in mind–body energetic awareness. It has no other purpose than to soothe, pamper, and nurture you. Like meditation, Harmony helps reduce your level of stress to create a feeling of peacefulness within your body.

Harmony is a bio-energetic healing exercise. It balances and harmonizes your brain and nervous system with the functional energies of your chakra system, enhancing communication. The seven body chakras and the eighth chakra, located one hand's length over your crown, form your second-most powerful energy system (your energetic bio-field, the energy that surrounds you, being the most powerful). The chakras vibrate with the tones of the musical scale, the eighth chakra vibrating at high-C and the root chakra vibrating at low-C. In this case, high-C ends one eight-note scale and begins another, thus connecting itself harmonically with the chakras above our crown and maintaining a continuous flow of Creation energy into our body.

Chakra System—Associated Tone on Musical Scale

8th Chakra / Godhead:	C	The First of the Spiritual Chakras
7th Chakra / Crown:	B	Pineal Glad
6th Chakra / Brow:	A	Pituitary
5th Chakra / Throat:	G	Thyroid
4th Chakra / Heart:	F	Thymus
3rd Chakra / Solar Plexus:	E	Pancreas–Spleen
2nd Chakra / Sacral:	D	Gonads–Ovaries
1st Chakra / Root:	C	Adrenal

This exercise incorporates the two neurovascular stress points on your forehead (Bladder, Gall Bladder, and Triple Warmer meridians; Governing Vessel; and the brow chakra are located in the area where your hand rests), the two at your occipital lobe (Bladder and Gall Bladder Meridians, and Governing Vessel), and because of location, includes your brain stem. This is a powerful energetic hold. Each of your seven body chakras and the eighth chakra over your crown are part of the exercise. You first address your neurovascular points by placing your hands over both the front and back points in a hold called The Occipital Hold. Then with your left hand over the neurovascular stress points at the back of your head, you begin to use your right hand to balance each individual chakra.

Occipital Hold

Graphic by Kirtan Coan

The Occipital Hold, an energetic hold taught by many energy healing systems, simultaneously stimulates relaxation and emotional release by creating positive physical change. Here is what happens when the neurovascular points are held. The neurovascular points on your forehead help restore normal blood flow (vascular flow) by reversing the fight-or-flight extra blood flow sent to your limbs. The neurovascular points at the occipital ridge help release your fears. Because your left or right hand is always at your brain stem, incorporating the neurovascular points, you positively encourage your ANS to return to the rest–digest response. Along the brain stem you also engage the Reticular Formation, a neural network within the Medulla that helps regulate sleep and attention. The Medulla also regulates your heart rate, breathing, and blood pressure, while the Pons, among other things, supports healthy sleep, breathing, swallowing, bladder control, and equilibrium. The Midbrain influences voluntary motor functioning (*Clinical Autonomic Disorders*, Phillip A. Low and Eduardo E. Benarroch 2008. *Energy Medicine*, Donna Eden and David Feinstein, PhD, 2008).

HUMAN BRAIN

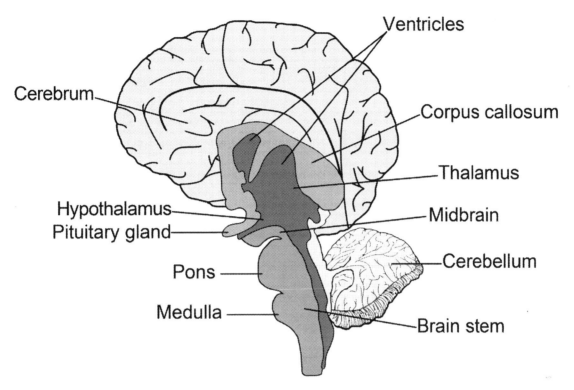

© Can Stock Photo Inc. / roxanabalint

The chakras are arranged vertically along your mid-line, front, and back body. The chakras correlate with the Central Vessel along your front mid-line and the Governing Vessel that flows along the spinal column. Your spinal chord's network of nerves reaches out from the spinal column like limbs on a tree, feeding every aspect of your body, including your organs. Each chakra feeds a specific area of your body, supplying essential life-giving energy. So, for example, if your third chakra is malfunctioning, the organs and glands of that chakra (Stomach, Liver, Gall Bladder, Spleen and Pancreas) are either provided an overabundance of energy or are suffering from an insufficiency. When we balance our third chakra, it begins to spin in the right direction at the right speed, properly providing the body's energetic needs.

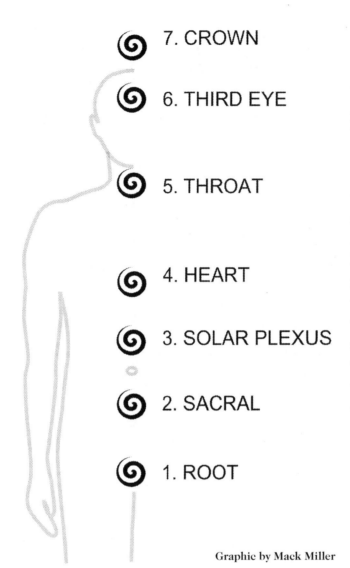

7. CROWN

6. THIRD EYE

5. THROAT

4. HEART

3. SOLAR PLEXUS

2. SACRAL

1. ROOT

Graphic by Mack Miller

I work with my body energetically every day, usually in a meditative way. One morning I was resting in bed working with the Reiki Harmony position (The Occipital Hold) to bring balance to my body because of a digestive upset and a viral cold. I asked my body to respond in a robust way. I wanted to enhance my sense of overall well-being and remain fully present, positive, and healthy. I listened to my body, followed my inner guidance, and the following energetic balance is the result. So: Let go, relax, let your muscles soften and your energy flow. This is a whole-body approach that will help you re-establish health and emotional well-being.

Directions for Harmony Mind–Body Energetic Exercise

The harmonizing function is done twice—once with your left hand over the occipital neurovascular points at the brain stem and your right hand working with each of the chakras, and once with your right hand on the same occipital neurovascular points at your brain stem and your left hand working with the chakras.

Forehead Neurovasuclar Points

Graphic by Kirtan Coan

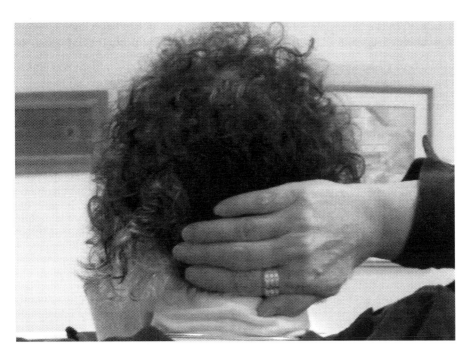

Occipital Lobe Neurovascular Points

Graphic by Kirtan Coan

- Recline in bed or on a couch. If you are using a pillow, it should be a thin pillow that allows good energy flow up and down your spinal column. Throughout the exercise, breathe from your belly: take nice, slow, deep breaths, inhaling and exhaling through your nose. The total exercise can be completed in 5 to 15 minutes, or you can enjoy the work as long as you like.
- Use the front-body chakra points as pictured in the chakra illustration.
- Breathe at least 3 balancing breaths at each of the seven chakras and at the eighth chakra located one hand's length above your crown. Chakras mimic an eight-note octave, with low-C and high-C being both the end of one scale and the beginning of the next. The eighth chakra is then the end of the body chakras and the beginning of the next group of chakras that continue above your head.
- Begin with your left hand at your occipital neurovascular points at your brain stem and your right hand at your brow chakra. Move your hand down your body, one chakra at a time, ending at the root chakra—then reverse the process moving up your body one chakra at time, ending at your crown chakra.
- Reverse hands. Your right hand is resting on your occipital neurovascular points at your brain stem and your left hand is balancing each of the chakras. Beginning at your brow chakra, breathe and balance each chakra as you move down your body, then breathe and balance each chakra, moving up your body and ending at your crown chakra. Then with your right hand remaining on your occipital neurovascular point at your brain stem, hold your left hand one hand's length over your crown chakra and breathe at least three times to make contact with and balance your eighth chakra. Including the eighth chakra as you end the exercise incorporates high-C, and the chakra system that continues into your energy field (bio-field). The chakras continue past the seven body chakras, upward through your bio-field, and downward from your root chakra to the foot chakras that receive energy from the Earth.

Harmony Mind–Body Energetic Balance is completed. Rest quietly for a moment or two, appreciating how good you feel. This is a great energetic balance to work with when you are physically and emotionally tired, not feeling well, or unable to sleep. It is available as a recording at www.mindfulpathways.com and can be downloaded as an MP3.

CHAPTER 4

The Nurturing Wellness Through Radical Self-Care Program: Before You Begin

Remember: Love and respect who you are today: honor the circumstances of your life; honor your level of physical, emotional, and spiritual health. Above all, remain patient and positive.

Creating a New Normal

Fight or flight is a basic physiological response that is wired into our minds and bodies for the purpose of preserving life. Your body goes into preservation mode with a programmed list of responses: Nerve cells fire, stress hormones are released into the blood stream, respiration rate increases; blood is redirected away from the digestive tract and into muscles, arms, and legs so you can run or fight. You become hyper aware, and your perception of pain diminishes. You are prepared for the enemy and are in attack mode. In this state you are not in touch with your rational mind and normal daily beliefs because you have to have quick instinctive action for survival. I know you have heard stories of heroic acts and superhuman feats accomplished in emergency situations. These acts are classic fight-or-flight responses. Chronic anxiety and stress sufferers stay in fight or flight and have many of the markers listed above ("The Fight or Flight Response," www.thebodysoulconnection.com/EducationCenter/fight.html, Dr. Neil F. Neimark, MD, University of California, Irvine).

The average person spends far too much time in emergency mode. Because of personal history, family responsibilities, family genetics, appointments, overwork, due dates, deadlines, personal illnesses, known and unknown environmental stressors, and financial challenges, we never deactivate our acute stress response. If you consider the negative effects of daily emotional stress coupled with the effects of all the various stressors you've experienced over your lifetime, it is easy to understand why your body is overworked, stays in fight or flight, and becomes exhausted.

Your work with REB and the Nurturing Wellness Through Radical Self-Care Program increases the amount of time you are in a calm, relaxed state and reduces the amount of time you spend in fight or flight. Calm, inner quiet allows positive change to begin deep within your body. You can be assured of long-term positive transformation as you acquire very powerful self-help skills and new positive attitudes that allow you to flow from emergency mode to relaxation mode in a natural, fluid manner.

REB is a powerful, comprehensive, and life-changing self-help tool. It creates positive inner emotional–physical change. The Nurturing Wellness Through Radical Self-Care Program is safe for everyone, even those who are very sensitive to inner change, as long as the guidelines are respected and followed. Individuals with severe and chronic anxiety (especially those who panic easily), post-traumatic stress disorder (PTSD), and rapid cycling bipolar disorder are asked to read the following paragraphs carefully because you *are* very sensitive to inner change. As you start this program, you begin to unwind a negative chain of events and your emotional response to those events. This is true for you and for all people who work the program.

REB is an exceptional modality for individuals with post-traumatic stress disorder. REB contains the bilateral elements of EMDR, a therapeutic in-office technique used to move you rapidly through trauma. The bilateral stimulation, as used with REB, accelerates emotional release and simultaneously creates a state of inner balance, relaxation and calm. It connects you with feelings of well-being and encourages your autonomic nervous system to function as it was designed to function. If you have been diagnosed with PTSD and your issues are unresolved, you have not felt inner calm and balance for a long time. It is necessary that you begin your work slowly, gaining confidence in the Nurturing Wellness Program and your ability to use it. Make sure you tell your mental health professional (if you have one) of your plans before you begin working with this program. If you and your therapist are working with EMDR, *do not* use the bilateral stimulation elements of REB (you'll learn more about them later) during your Nurturing Wellness Program.

If you suspect you have PTSD and you are not in therapy, or in therapy and not working with EMDR, the guidelines are different. First use REB as a relaxation technique, staying in the posture for up to three minute at a time so you have the opportunity to adjust gradually to the positive physical–emotional change it creates. Once you have practiced resting in the posture you can begin to use Mindful Meditation with REB. It is safe to use the affirmations and the active release elements of REB when you and your body are familiar with the process, and you are used to the deep relaxation that occurs. As you begin to work with the affirmations, go slowly and work with only one or two affirmations at a time. As you begin to understand the power of the process, you can increase the number of affirmations you work with and increase the length of time you stay in the posture. If you are part of a Nurturing Wellness Through Radical Self-Care group, stay in contact with your facilitator. Go to page 90 and review the Readiness affirmations so you understand the program more fully.

If you have bipolar disorder, especially rapid cycling bipolar disorder, read this paragraph carefully. If you have mood swings that shift often or suddenly and don't have a formal diagnosis, read this information with care. One of the effective non-medication therapeutic techniques used in the treatment of bipolar disorder is personal and environmental structure. Structure helps you create balance and routine, and both help you maintain mood stability. This program is ideal for bipolar disorder, but there are guidelines you must observe. Begin slowly, staying in the posture for one or two minutes. After resting in the posture a few times with success, you can begin to meditate using Mindful Meditation with REB. As your body becomes used to the relaxation and the internal changes that occur because you are relaxed, you are free to use the general guidelines of the program. The key is to progress slowly, use the meditations often, and keep your list of affirmations short. Always remember to tell your professional mental health team about your work and your progress.

Let me give you an example. A woman with PTSD and non-medicated rapid cycling bipolar was in one of my first groups. She wanted to use REB because she felt it would help her, and I agreed. The first time she tried REB, she became agitated and challenged. She was emotionally unprepared for the inner quiet she felt, and she was stunned by the emotional gains, even with the first use in group. She called me the day after group and we talked. This first response did not mean she couldn't use the program. It did mean her mind and body had to adjust to REB, and she needed to approach the process slowly. She followed directions and gradually worked into the full program. Once she understood and accepted the physical–emotional shifts, she prospered! She made tremendous progress and felt wonderful about her ability to self-regulate, self-soothe, and relax deeply.

If you have chronic, severe anxiety with or without panic, your body is energetically and physically distressed and exhausted due to months or years of being in fight or flight. In this condition, most people either hesitate to recognize change no matter how evident, or they notice the tiniest change that occurs within their body and become more anxious because of it. I've known women who could feel an egg leave their ovary. There are men and women who are so sensitive they can "feel" the seasons begin to change, and the "feeling" heightens anxiety. Because of feelings or physiological sensations that are sudden and the fear of the unknown it is important to go slowly with REB and this program. Once you realize you are safe, you will prosper.

A woman with severe, long-term anxiety and panic was in my office learning to stop her severe panic attacks. We knew each other well and there was a great deal of mutual trust. She sat back and elevated her legs to the ottoman in my office. She sat in the REB posture for a couple of minutes, beginning to relax and breathe more slowly. As soon as she felt the first change that signaled relaxation, she became frightened and began to have a significant panic attack. I softly suggested she stay in the posture, continuing to use the bilateral squeezing so she could work through her fear. She did, and I gently assured her she was safe. In just a few seconds her panic attack ended. In another 30 seconds she was smiling, stunned at the power of the posture and what she had accomplished. She became a believer and dramatically changed her life, accomplishing many things her fear had prevented: driving, flying, eating in public, a new romantic relationship.

Many of my clients have stopped panic attacks through regular use of the REB posture. Others have been able to lower their dose of powerful anxiety medications. The process has helped others navigate the bumpy waters of grief and loss, because it helped them balance the associated emotions and freed them to move forward with life. The REB posture has helped many people fall asleep at night without the aid of medications and helped them get back to sleep if they happened to awaken during the night.

Recovery takes time and effort. As you resolve the emotions around a specific life situation or event, your anxiety, worries, and concerns decrease and your symptoms become less acute. The reduction of your overall stress load allows healing to begin. As you get healthier, the memories become less influential, and you begin to attract healthier, happier people into your inner circle. Attitudes and behaviors you once tolerated are no longer acceptable. You are able to set healthier emotional boundaries. You are able to think about your challenging experience without emotional arousal. The more positive thoughts and emotions you add to your physical, emotional, spiritual energy body, the harder it is to hold onto negative thoughts and emotions.

The affirmations in this program reinforce the positive feelings and beliefs you already have. The positive language stimulates the release of negative thoughts, beliefs, feelings, and events by pointing out the distance between a positive belief system and what you currently feel and believe. I encourage you to welcome all of your feelings so you are able to allow the REB Nurturing Wellness process to alleviate conscious and unconscious negativity. Allowing is important. Remaining a witness during each session, rather than trying too hard or becoming judgmental of your success, is important. To succeed you don't have to do anything but stay in the posture until the negative feelings subside. Once a feeling subsides, it is gone forever. Your emotional load is lightened. Appreciate the small changes. Celebrate the growth you make during each session.

Remaining a Witness During Your Session

As a witness you are an observer and unattached to the outcome even though you may have created a desired outcome. You accept with gratitude the feelings, emotions or sensations as they arise. Allow them to flow through you, knowing you are nurturing your own wellness.

Now is a good time to introduce you to the benefits you can expect to achieve as you balance your ANS, your physical body and emotions. Few people have a balanced autonomic nervous system. Most people don't know what the ANS is, and therefore don't know how it works or how to repair its functioning. Because you have chosen to read this book and work the Nurturing Wellness program, you are well on your way to understanding the workings of your body and making the positive changes you desire.

A healthy, balanced autonomic nervous system is your very best health asset. As you begin the Nurturing Wellness Program, you begin to create a new emotional and physical normal. I suggest you mark the attributes that are most important to you. They are another road map, or guidance system, as you begin to feel healthier and happier.

- Good, restful, rejuvenating sleep
- The ability to relax and rest easily and efficiently
- The ability to perform at optimal levels during an emergency
- Resilience in the presence of stress, shock, accident, or trauma
- Good digestion, including healthy, normal daily elimination
- Good peristalsis in the intestinal track
- Normal production and elimination of urine
- A strong immune system
- A steady, strong heartbeat, rate, and rhythm
- Normal dilation of your pupils
- Good, normal perspiration
- Balanced hormones
- A good, healthy libido
- Regulated blood sugar
- Normal blood pressure
- Normal thyroid gland function
- Tendency to heal easily and quickly from an accident, wound, or surgery
- Enjoyment of life as a calm, peaceful, contented person
- Clear, reality-based thinking and good decision making
- Normal impulse control
- Positive thought followed by positive action
- Consistent self-regulation of moods
- Good cooperation between all the systems of the body for optimal functioning

After you have completed the 12-week program, you can change the words a bit and use the listed items as affirmations, combining them with the REB posture. As you meditate in the REB posture, allow the energy of each item to flow through your entire mind–body–spirit system, filling your heart and soul with all the wonderful benefits they offer. Breathe them in. Circulate them through your whole body. Nourish yourself emotionally and spiritually, one item at a time. Rejuvenate. Live longer.

Beginning on page 211 you'll find instructions on how to use REB to prevent anxiety and panic attacks. There are instructions to help you improve your ability to sleep soundly and wake up feeling refreshed and rested. You'll learn how to take REB to the dentist or doctor's office, using the posture to help you manage stress related to medical procedures and interventions. You'll also find instructions on how to recover from phobias.

You are truly engaged in a magnificent opportunity to make the positive changes you've longed for. Many of the concepts and strategies may be new to you. Western lifestyle is often a fast-paced 'get it done' way of life. We take a lot of things for granted or just expect to "pick up" coping skills as we go along. However, it usually does not work that way. We have to learn life skills at home, at school, through religious instruction and through social interactions in organized clubs like boy and girl scouts or via organized sports. As children, few of us were intentionally taught emotional self-care, so for most of us it is a new concept. Another new term is spiritual self-care which relates to our belief system, our worthiness, finding and nurturing a sense of connection, and discovering a deeper meaning in life. Both forms of self-care are as essential as learning to brush our teeth, yet they are often overlooked or taken for granted. Many of us were never exposed to positive structure and positive boundaries. We have to learn what they are and learn to apply them to our life as adults. This book gives you the opportunity to learn skills you might have missed along the way and exposes you to information and methods that help you *heal* your life, skills that bring confidence into your life and create a feeling of safety.

Fine-Tuning the REB Posture

Comfort is essential. Sit or recline in a position that allows you to breathe from your belly in a naturally deep manner. Breathe naturally from the belly. Inhale and exhale through your nose as this boosts your autonomic nervous system response (www.rebprotocol.net, Phillip Warren).

How to Do Belly Breathing

If you watch an infant breathing, you'll notice that his or her little tummy goes up and down with each *in* and *out* breath. To begin breathing from your abdomen the way you breathed as an infant and small child, hold a hand on your abdomen so you can feel your belly expanding on the *in* breath and flattening on the *out* breath. Take a nice, deep breath and allow that breath to fall into your belly with the exhale. Pause. On the next inhale, begin to breathe deeply and naturally from your belly.

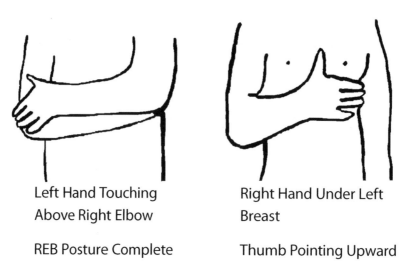

Left Hand Touching
Above Right Elbow

REB Posture Complete

Right Hand Under Left
Breast

Thumb Pointing Upward

www.rebprotocol.net

For best results, plan for a few uninterrupted minutes. No TV. Soft relaxation music is OK and may help quiet your body and mind. If you use relaxation music, make sure the music is played softly, has no vocal elements and all the segments are peaceful with no sudden change in rhythm or sound. To use the REB posture, your right arm rests across the front of the body with the hand resting softly under your left breast engaging your Spleen meridian. The left arm crosses over the right arm and your left hand rests on top of your right arm just about an inch above the elbow, engaging your Triple Warmer meridian. You may hook your left thumb under your right arm for stability. This holds your hand solidly in just the right place for optimal success. Place your tongue on the gum ridge behind your upper teeth. This connects your Central and Governing Vessels and keeps your energy flowing smoothly in an arc called the Microcosmic Orbit. Your ankles are crossed. You can move them right over left or left over right anytime you choose. Crossing or uncrossing your ankles will not lessen the positive effect of the balance. (Find definitions of **Central Vessel, Governing Vessel, Spleen,** and **Triple Warmer** in the glossary beginning on page 221.)

When simply resting in the posture, using it for relaxation, an afternoon pick-me-up, or getting ready for sleep, close your eyes and begin to notice yourself noticing your relaxation process. You are a witness to your own relaxation. If you notice areas of stress, acknowledge them, and continue to rest. Rather than interacting with the stress or getting angry with yourself, which slows down or stops your relaxation response, simply noticing works best. If you simply notice the stress and continue to rest in the posture, your body will do its very best to resolve it. Witnessing is a mindfulness skill. You mindfully notice and accept yourself and your level of stress as it is at this moment, yet continue to rest and relax. If you notice a negative thought, idea, or belief, or begin to think about all you have to do, acknowledge your thought, label it (worry, anger, memory, fear, etc.), accept yourself as you are at this moment, then let go of the thought and continue to rest and relax.

Other Relevant REB Information

Healing your autonomic nervous system does not happen instantly, but over a period of time you will find you simply feel better. REB balances emotions tied to past worries and calms your fears of the future. In other words, it helps you stay "now" focused. You begin to live life in the present moment. Everyone has a relaxation response built into their body. We lose that response because chronic stress and anxiety exhausts various systems of the body, rendering them less effective and sometimes ineffective. The posture helps you find and restore your automatic relaxation response. Once this response is fully developed, the posture itself becomes a cue to relax. You'll notice that as soon as you think "posture" you begin to feel stress and tension drain from your body. You'll realize that you can use it anytime and anywhere to maintain relaxation, emotional balance and heightened awareness. You can take the posture to the dentist, to the delivery room, to a chemotherapy appointment, to a tense office meeting, on a walk in the woods, into your morning shower, or into a nice, warm, relaxing bubble bath.

I know the greatest benefit of REB is the simultaneous emotional balancing and release that occurs while resting in the posture. Years ago a young pregnant woman was referred to my office by her midwife. She was in the midst of a high-risk pregnancy complicated by exceptionally high stress levels. She was experiencing flash backs of a traumatic event and having severe panic attacks that threatened the health of her baby and the pregnancy. I taught her the REB posture and relaxation process during her first appointment simply to keep her safe during the intake. At each subsequent appointment she engaged the posture at the beginning of each therapy session and remained in the posture whenever she discussed the trauma or the fear she felt for her unborn child. The posture created emotional release and balanced negative, painful emotions as she told her story. We kept the stress at a safe level throughout her therapy and stopped the panic attacks without medication. A few months later she successfully delivered a beautiful, healthy baby.

The young mother leaned to relax deeply and notice her responses from a more distant witness perspective, rather than from the emotional anxiety-filled perspective she was used to experiencing. She was able to bring her mind–body system back into a reasonable balance and safely deliver her baby. The ability to regain your inner balance is a magnificent gift you can give to yourself. Imagine the benefits of remembering a trauma and no longer going into fight or flight. Imagine sitting down to eat a holiday meal without feeling panic about the menu or the length of time you'll be exposed to food and food-related conversation. Imagine thinking of your mother's illness and death without crying or worrying about all the things you didn't get done or anguishing about the relationship you wish the two of you could have shared. Imagine feeling comfortable in your own body 24/7 and living more confidently and securely every day.

Releasing Unwanted Negativity and Stress

REB's Primary Release Technique: Bilateral, Rhythmic Squeezing

When resting in the REB posture, relaxing, breathing deeply and normally through your nose, begin a bilateral (left to right) rhythmic squeeze. Your left hand gently squeezes your right arm where your left hand is resting. Then your right hand squeezes your left chest area under your breast where you right hand is resting. The squeeze is very gentle, and need be little more than a touch. This right-to-left rhythmic movement increases your ability to release unwanted thoughts, ideas, beliefs, and stored negativity. It helps to move stress out of your physical body, including your nervous system.

The kind of release stimulated by the technique above goes far beyond the release of stress that you experience when meditating with the REB posture. The bilateral squeezing gives you the opportunity to let go of long standing issues, situations and traumas that disturb your entire mind–body–spirit system. Along with the other REB strategies, it allows you to release unnamed stressors that create the kind of anxiety that ultimately leads some people to adopt self-sabotaging behaviors like compulsive spending, emotional eating, alcoholism, work addiction, and self-inflicted injurious behaviors like cutting.

If you are completely mentally and emotionally exhausted by your current life circumstance you can benefit greatly from all of the REB release techniques. The possibilities for real growth are limitless. Remember to spend your first week doing nothing but resting and rejuvenating with meditation. Once you begin using the release techniques, it is essential that you follow directions in order to avoid causing a rush of feelings that can disrupt your progress.

Embracing Change

Many people with a bipolar diagnosis also have post-traumatic stress disorder. If you happen to have a bipolar diagnosis, suffer from post-traumatic stress disorder, and have consulted your mental health professional and are *not* being treated by Eye Movement Desensitization and Reprocessing (EMDR), begin your Nurturing Wellness Program with Mindful Meditation using REB. Once you feel confident with the meditation, you can begin the REB bilateral release slowly with sessions of no more than 1 to 3 minutes. After several days of 1 to 3 minute sessions, slowly increase your time using the bilateral squeezing. Once you establish this pattern and feel secure in the technique, and are used to the changing body sensations, you can move forward with confidence.

For those with long-standing, severe worry, anxiety, and stress, your body has to become accustomed to the feelings associated with relaxation. When I talk with clients in my office, I notice confusion between experiencing an enjoyable activity that *distracts* the mind for a brief time and deep relaxation that *quiets* the mind, reduces muscle tension, reduces the flow of adrenaline, and creates an overall feeling of well-being. I'll share examples of this kind of misunderstanding with you.

A middle-aged male client experiencing panic attacks told me about the "deeply relaxing" routine he enjoyed in the evenings after work. He sits down in front of the TV and turns on CNN, hooks up his computer and watches a video, plays a game, answers email, and plays on Facebook and Twitter. If he is really wound up, he adds a beer or a glass of wine to his routine. He swears this relaxes him and that he feels better after about an hour. He has successfully distracted himself, taken his mind off his work problems, and engaged in activities he enjoys. Yet, his mind is still active and he remains overstimulated. He might feel better because he has enjoyed a rather mindless hour, but his routine does not provide deep, healing relaxation. His routine is habitual, self-soothing activity. There is a huge difference between an anxiety-busting, mindful, physically restorative experience and an activity that temporarily distracts you to alleviate situational stress.

An elderly woman came into my office to see if she could learn to reduce anxiety and feel better. She complained of nervousness and trembling, especially in the early morning. She said she had a "relaxation routine" she engaged in upon awakening, and was upset because she was unable to reduce her anxiety medication. When asked to describe her routine she told this story: I get up in the morning and go to the kitchen. It is usually quiet because I am the only one up. I brew a pot of coffee and then sit down and drink a cup or two while I smoke a cigarette. I really enjoy this routine. I might have a slice of buttered toast with the coffee. After the coffee and cigarette, I take my Xanax and have another cup of coffee and read the newspaper. I don't think my medication is working. Do you think you can help me? I told her yes, I could help, and explained how her morning activities were actually supporting her anxiety issues rather than calming her. She was eating little or no food, spending an hour reading local news and filling her body with caffeine and nicotine, topped off by an addictive benzodiazepine (Xanax). The only relaxing elements in her morning routine were the quiet environment in her kitchen and the familiarity of repetitive activity. Her muscles remained tense, her mind filled with local accidents and recent deaths, and her nervous system stimulated by the coffee and cigarettes.

The relaxation response feels "foreign" to individuals like my clients above. It has been years since either of them has experienced a naturally generated deep relaxation response. While relaxation is wanted and welcomed at one level, a full and deep mind–body relaxation might be startling to them. It is important to be consciously aware of what relaxation feels like prior to any activity that induces deep mind–body relaxation. Instead of being fearful, you want to eagerly accept the feelings of relaxation for what they are: your friend and ally.

Relaxation often produces regular breathing that is deeper than your normal breathing. You can feel the change occur in your body as you realize your chest muscles have opened up allowing a deeper breath. You might experience a feeling of physical lightness, a change in body temperature, tingling throughout your body, a heavy weighted feeling, or feel as if you are sinking into the couch or massage table. Accompanying the physical feelings are emotional changes like increased hopefulness, a sense of well-being, a sense of self-knowledge and self-worth, reality-based insight and mental clarity, and occasionally a giggle of excitement accompanied by a sigh of relief! If the weighty feeling happens, know that it is a normal muscular response for some people.

I was in a Tai Chi class the first time my chest muscles fully relaxed. As they relaxed, my chest and shoulders felt very heavy. The weight felt like pressure, and I felt some concern. Slowly I realized I was experiencing a profound change in muscle tension. I became excited, and astounded, by the level of stress I had been carrying opposed to the complete relaxation I was feeling as I rested in a standing qi gong posture. It was a life-affirming mind–body experience, and I greatly valued knowing that I had the ability to recreate the relaxation. The experience I had in my Tai Chi class is very similar to the experience you can have with REB. REB allows you to develop your relaxation response, which is a built-in ability to automatically flow from a high-stress situation into a naturally relaxed state of being. You are 100% safe in the REB posture and with the benefits of deep, life-enhancing relaxation.

Some of you may have the fear that if you relax, you'll lose control of a troubling situation, lose control of yourself, or your motivation will be decreased, resulting in something bad happening. This kind of thinking is called a psychological reversal. This means that your stress level, anxiety, and fear have caused you to reverse a thought, creating an internal conundrum ("Energy Psychology Interactive," http://theamt.com/psychological_reversal. htm. David Feinstein). Research has shown that an individual's mental acuity, motivation, and overall awareness are increased when relaxed. That means your performance in sports and daily life actually increases when you are relaxed and your autonomic nervous system is balanced. The REB Nurturing Wellness Through Radical Self-Care Program takes into consideration the most common psychological reversals. If you stick with the program your thought processes will correct themselves, and you will become more positive and confident.

Other Release Techniques

There are a few people who are distracted by the rhythmic, bilateral squeezing that accelerates the REB release process. If you discover you are one of them, try gently swaying left to right while you hold the REB posture. Sway gently to the left, then gently to the right in a nice, slow motion. Swaying works better for some people, and the results using side-to-side swaying are excellent. Please note that rocking front to back will not produce the same results.

The release technique I'm going to mention now, combined with the REB posture, can be very productive—especially if you are not using the bilateral squeezing or swaying. It can also be added to the bilateral squeezing or swaying. As you sit resting in the posture, create a yawn and blink your eyes several times. For some, these two activities stimulate the release of unwanted negative thoughts and beliefs. In fact, yawning and eye blinking often occur naturally while you are in the posture. This is normal, and the yawning and blinking end after you disengage the posture. In fact, involuntary yawning and blinking are signs that your work is making a positive difference in your life! Yawning? What a great opportunity for an unscheduled nap!

You'll be ending each of your daily release sessions with a Heart Massage, an energy-balancing technique I learned from Dr. Barbara Stone, author of *Invisible Roots* (2008). The Heart Massage is a quick and comforting way to balance your energy field, ending your REB session with positive heart-centered feelings. The Heart Massage is wonderful for daily self-care, creating relaxation and peacefulness. The general directions are below. I use this brief activity every day, multiple times each day.

Fine-Tuning the Heart Massage

Place your right hand in the middle of your chest, right above your breasts. Your fingers are pointing to the left and you'll be circling your hand left to right. Circle your hand in a clockwise direction. To get the motion right, visualize the face of the clock with the back of the clock touching your chest, the face looking out from your body. Your hand is resting at your heart center, fingers pointing to 3:00. Your hand circles to the left, moves down to 6:00, around and up to the right at 9:00 and back to center at 12:00. Continue circling. Adding an affirmation is very healing.

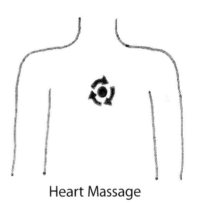

Heart Massage

Courtesy of Dr. Barbara Stone
Graphic by Jennifer Robinett

- Along with a positive statement, use a Heart Massage when you want to feel good and as a way to say thank you to your body: "Thank you, body, for supporting my life so well. I love feeling happy. You are magnificent!"
- Use it with a pep-up statement: "Thank you, body, for your support. I have faith in us to get the job done."
- You may use it at bedtime to help prepare for sleep: "I am ready for sleep. I look forward to feeling rested and restored in the morning."
- Use it if you are upset about something and want to bring yourself into balance and think more clearly: "Even though I am upset (about XYZ), I deeply and completely love, accept, and forgive myself. There is so much I can learn from this situation."

The Affirmations and REB

Radiant Energies Balance is a meridian–Radiant Circuit-based energy psychology, and it will help your personal growth work if you understand more about how the meridians and Radiant Circuits function. You can add to the brief explanation below by once again reviewing the information on page 17 where I mention that the Radiant Circuits are also known as the Circuits of Joy and list some of the positive results you are likely to achieve by engaging them. The health and wellness information is very inspirational as you embark on your Nurturing Wellness Journey.

Meridians: There are 12 primary meridians in the body flowing energy (chi) within closed vessels, much like blood flows within our veins. The meridians adjust metabolism, remove blockages, and help determine the speed and form of cellular change. Without their flow of energy, there is no life. They affect every organ and every system in the body: immune, nervous, endocrine, circulatory, respiratory, digestive, skeletal, muscular, and lymphatic (http://www.innersource.net/em/. *Energy Medicine,* Donna Eden and David Feinstein, PhD 1999 and *Energy Medicine for Women,* Donna Eden and David Feinstein, PhD 2008).

Radiant Circuits: Radiant circuits operate as fluid fields, with a distinct and spontaneous intelligence. They work like little computer hyperlinks, jumping quickly to where they are needed, providing feelings of joy and spiritual connection along with feelings of vitality. The Triple Warmer meridian acts as a mobilizer, getting you ready for whatever is needed; the Spleen meridian acts as a calming energy, providing you with healing warmth and calmness, lifting your morale (http://www.innersource.net/em). *Energy Medicine,* Donna Eden and David Feinstein, PhD 1999 and *Energy Medicine for Women,* Donna Eden and David Feinstein, PhD 2008).

Meridian functioning affects our emotional health. John Diamond, MD, a physician prominent in the field of Energy Psychology, has worked for years pairing the meridians with specific emotional characteristics. For example, the Spleen meridian is the meridian of confidence (balance and acceptance). The affirmation he suggests is, "I have faith and confidence in my future." When we are engaged in the REB posture, repeating the affirmation and using active release, we are clearing issues and the associated emotions that have kept us from feeling, "I have faith and confidence in my future." As we remove these negative emotions and the issues they have created, we can assume we have created a new emotional response that will exhibit in day-to-day life. We also assume that clearing has corrected energy flow within the meridian, which enables the meridian to be more efficient in the distribution of energy and energy information. The new emotional attitude and the corrected energy flow reduces stress in the body, increasing overall body functioning. This same scenario occurs each time you complete your Nurturing Wellness Through Radical Self-Care daily release session. Your possibilities for creating health and well-being are limitless. You can find quick access to Dr. Diamond's work at www.drjohndiamond.com. If you want to learn more, you can read some of his many books: *Life Energy* (1998), *Your Body Doesn't Lie* (1989), and his newest, *Freedom from Fear,* published in 2011.

The Readiness affirmations list is designed to help correct psychological reversals, faulty or reversed thoughts, and prepare you for the rest of the program. Removing these emotional blocks creates new emotional opportunities for growth and change. Most everyone has at least one psychological reversal and most people have quite a few. An example of a psychological reversal is "No matter what I do or how hard I try, I'll never get over this depression." The more reversals we can correct, the greater the possibility of good emotional and physical health.
Energy psychologists: Use a SUDS level and muscle testing to monitor progress.

Directions for Affirmations and REB
During the first week (or the second week if you are using the alternate program), you'll be working only with the Readiness Affirmations. You can work with the whole list or begin with two or three that you know are problematic or hard to say. If you are thinking "I just don't believe what I am saying and I can't speak these words," feel free to modify the affirmations using words you can say. Belief in what you are saying increases the effectiveness of your work. After a day or two working with the modified affirmation, try saying the original words again. If you still feel uncomfortable with the original words, modify the affirmation a second time, bringing the words closer to the original version. You'll use this strategy with the Readiness Affirmations and all the other affirmations in the Nurturing Wellness Through Radical Self-Care Program.

Modifying your affirmations
"I am worthy of good mind–body–spirit health and well-being,"
   might become
"Health is very important, and I choose to feel positive,"
   might become
"I am a worthy person, and I choose to be healthy,"

Remember, Rome was not built in a day. However, by the end of your first week combining the affirmations with REB, you'll be more hopeful no matter what is going on in your life. At the end of the week, if you feel you are not ready to leave the Readiness Affirmations, don't. Your body–mind–spirit system knows exactly what you need. Some people choose to stay with Readiness for several weeks and others will keep one or more of the Readiness affirmations during the whole program.

After each daily session, fill out the self-evaluation on the **Nurturing Wellness Journal Page**. The Journal Pages are so very important to your growth during the program. This page helps you focus on the positive changes you're making and allows you to keep a clear view of your goals. The page provides much-needed structure. Take a look at the first **Nurturing Wellness Journal Page** on page 109 and familiarize yourself with the content.

Various physical and emotional responses can occur with any kind of energy psychology or energy healing work because of the energetic shifts. Some people feel energized and very positive and sleep more soundly than usual. Some people notice some subtle differences after a session, and these may vary from day to day. Some have absolutely no *felt* response, as the shifts are below conscious awareness. Others experience some feelings of tiredness or even feelings of unease and agitation as they go through the week. All these responses are normal. The ability to "feel" energetic shifts and physical–emotional results vary from person to person. If you are a person who feels the energy, the feelings become a motivation to continue. For those who never feel energetic shifts, there is danger in thinking the program is not working for you. It is, be patient. Here is a true story about working hard, with no felt sense that anything is happening.

A young woman with a life-threatening illness was receiving energy healing work and treatment for anxiety. She'd suffered for years with anxiety and it was complicating her life, especially now, because of her illness. She was struggling to make the needed personal changes, to slow down and take care of her physical body and her emotions. Following her doctor's orders to make and keep appointments for energy healing and energy psychology was the best she could do. Each appointment went about the same. She came, she participated, and went home. When she went to her doctor for a routine exam he told her the cancer site looked better than he had ever seen it. She still didn't believe anything was happening energetically because she couldn't "feel" it and she couldn't see the area of her body that was involved. She was skeptical and she couldn't believe her doctor! One day she came running into the office for her appointment, anxious to talk. I was sure there was something very, very wrong. She wanted to tell me about her toe. She had a fungus on a nail and always kept her toes polished because of it. For some reason she'd removed the polish and was able to see her natural nail. The fungus nail was growing out smooth, pink, and healthy. It was her "feeling." Something she could see and touch.

Change is occurring simply because you decided to complete the Nurturing Wellness Through Radical Self-Care Program. If you don't feel it, one day you will notice you responded differently to a stressor that usually sets you off. That will be your "felt sense" that you are making progress. For those of you who do feel tired and agitated at times, remember the feelings are temporary and the tiredness and agitation are your experiential indicator that you are making progress. If you are being stretched emotionally and there is too much unease and tiredness, I encourage you to first try to work through the feelings with the posture and active release. If that does not soothe you, take a day or two off or shorten your sessions so your body has the rest it needs to make the energetic adjustments it is working hard to make. When it does adjust, you will feel better physically and be glad you stuck it out.

Below is the journal page section that helps you work through an affirmation that is really bothering you, causing feelings to surface with the side effect of tiredness and agitation.

(Optional) Each day you have the option to choose one affirmation from your list for in-depth work.
Affirmation _____

Beginning **SUDS** level _____   Ending **SUDS** level _____

SUDS: Subjective Units of Distress
Rate your distress on a scale between 0 (low) and 10 (high). Aim to achieve an ending SUDS of 2 or below.

SUDS stands for subjective units of distress. You measure your distress on a scale of 0–10 with 0 meaning no distress and 10 meaning your distress is very high. Checking your progress by using the SUDS scale keeps you objective and gives you a measurement of progress that is easy to work with. You'll want to get your distress level down to at least a 2. At that level you will notice a huge positive change.

You are in control of your program and you make the decision about the level and quantity of work that is comfortable for you. Your attitude is everything. Letting go of the REB posture stops the release process immediately and you can let go anytime you want to. Letting go of the REB posture does not cause you to lose the gains you've just accomplished. It only stops the release so you can rest and relax. You are creating a new normal, and your positive attitude is helping you feel better emotionally and physically. Think about any release as a welcome friend, because that is exactly what it is. Release is a welcome friend.

I have an office client who gets a wave of nausea each time her body makes an energetic correction. She does not like the feeling, yet she looks forward to the brief wave of nausea because she knows when the session is over she is going to feel much better. Many people have little muscle twitches and spasms as they release energetic blocks. I happen to be a person that twitches, sometimes spasms, during energy work. I know when my body jerks and twitches during a session I am having a great day! I know I've let go of something that was disturbing my inner balance.

Choosing Affirmations that are Right for You

Fill out one **Nurturing Wellness Journal Page** for each day whether or not you work with the affirmations. Recording how you choose to use your daily rejuvenation time is very important, because you are learning what you need emotionally, physically, and spiritually. You are listening to your inner voice and following your own inner wisdom. Remember to use at least one day for meditation. It is helpful to use one of the meditations in the book because these are written especially for your Nurturing Wellness journey. It is my experience that a meditation recorded in my own voice (if the recording is well-done) is very meaningful. You can also download recordings at www.mindfulpathways.com.

From this point on you'll choose the affirmations that feel right for you. Each person has a different list of affirmations each week because each of us has our own wants, needs, goals, and life experiences. You can choose one affirmation from each list or choose to work with one of the categories. Keep the list you generate for the whole week, dropping one or two if you realize that you've chosen too many. The categories are not meant to be followed one after the other. Choosing a personally meaningful category of affirmations or choosing one or two affirmations from various categories actually supports your journey as you are choosing to work with what *you* need *now*.

Please remember to limit your weekly list to 15 affirmations. Any more is just too much stimulation for your mind–body–spirit system. Some of you will find that three to five affirmations are enough for you, while others will want more. The number of affirmations you choose within a week will not change the outcome of the Nurturing Wellness Through Radical Self-Care Program. Everyone makes progress. Some of us just simply feel more is better or have a belief that tells us to push forward regardless. Pushing forward just for the sake of pushing forward may be temporarily rewarding, but it will negatively impact your outcome by adding stress. Comfort is the key word. Relaxation and peace within is your goal. If you fear you won't get through all the affirmations by the end of the 90-day program, don't worry about it. You can continue working on your own after the 90 days. A good many of you will end up using parts of the Nurturing Wellness Through Radical Self-Care Program for years to come. Allowing yourself to move forward peacefully and wisely may be the most positive change you make.

Daily Release Work

Your work can be gentle using passive release, or your work can be active, using the REB emotional release technique. Passive release happens by setting a desired outcome, noticing your thoughts and body sensations, breathing and resting in the posture. Active release happens when you use bilateral squeezing or swaying. The directions below use bilateral squeezing or swaying. If you want a softer session, omit the squeezing and swaying. A typical release session without meditation lasts 10–15 minutes.

Have your workbook and a pen or pencil with you as you begin.

Fill out the pre-session section of your **Nurturing Wellness Journal Page:**

- Desired Outcome
- My Mood Today
- Gratitude for Today?

- Notice what you are feeling and thinking before you begin and make a note of it.
- Affirmations you'll be using today

Some people like to meditate before they do their daily work, feeling it creates better success. If you are one of them, listen to your meditation now.

Decide if you are going to work with passive release or active release.

Work at a comfortable speed, giving yourself time to process the work you are doing.

Engage the REB Relaxation Posture and begin to relax. Remember to place your tongue on the gum ridge behind your upper teeth. Breathe from your abdomen and through your nose. Take all the time you need.

- Notice when the relaxation begins to soothe your body.
- Once you feel the relaxation, begin the bilateral squeezing or swaying.

While engaged in the release work, read the first affirmation on your list. Pause after reading it. Remain in the posture. Take a naturally deep breath. Read the affirmation a second time. Pause, and take a naturally deep breath.

- Fill out the "After the session I noticed" section on your **Nurturing Wellness Journal Page** and complete the page.
- Repeat the steps above for each affirmation on your list.
- When you have completed your list of affirmations, fill out "After the session I noticed." If one affirmation created strong emotion for you, you can choose to work on it now using the directions on the journal page.
- When all work is completed, fill out the "I noticed that my daily sessions are creating positive changes" portion of the sheet.
- Many people have a lot to say after their session. Write down anything you want to remember. Insights don't stay with you, even though you think they will. Use **Today's Insights** pages for your weekly logs.
- Use a **Heart Massage** to say "Thank You" to you for doing the work today. Say "Thank You" to your mind and body for working in harmony with you. Say "Thank You" for whatever is in your heart.

Structuring Your 12-Week Program

Nurturing Wellness Through Radical Self-Care is designed to be flexible so your individual needs are met. You design your weekly program. All the options create success, so choose the option that is right for you this week, knowing you can choose differently next week.

1st Week

- Follow the directions for pairing REB with Affirmations.
- Use only the Readiness Affirmations this week.
- At least one day of meditation using the meditations designed for the program.
- Complete the **Journal Page** and **Self-Care First!** page.
- Begin your meditation journal.

1st Week Alternative

- A week of meditation using the meditations designed for the program.
- Complete the **Journal Page** and **Self-Care First!** page.
- Begin your meditation journal.

2nd Week through Week 12

- Design your own program using REB with Affirmations.
- You can continue to use some or all of the Readiness Affirmations throughout the program.
- Choose up to 15 affirmations from one category or mix and match from different categories.
- At least one meditation each week using the meditations designed for the program.
- Journal after meditation using your meditation journal.
- Complete the **Journal Page** and **Self-Care First!** page.

2nd Week through Week 12 Alternative

- Meditate each day.
- Design your own program using REB with Affirmations, feeling free to complete this activity on some days and not on others.
- You can continue using some or all of the Readiness Affirmations throughout the program.
- When using the affirmations, choose up to 15 affirmations from one category or mix and match from different categories. I suggest using 10 or less.
- Journal after meditation using your meditation journal.
- Complete the **Journal Page** and **Self-Care First!** page.

Stay positive. Relax. Restore. Rejuvenate. Create well-being!

PART 2

NURTURING WELLNESS
through
RADICAL SELF-CARE
WORKBOOK

CHAPTER 5

Eleven

Thirty spokes together make a wheel for a cart.

It is the empty space in the center

of the wheel which enables it to be used.

Mold clay into a vessel;

it is the emptiness within

that creates the usefulness of the vessel.

Cut out doors and windows in a house;

it is the empty space inside

that creates the usefulness of the house.

Thus, what we have may be something substantial,

But its usefulness lies in the unoccupied, empty space.

The substance of your body is enlivened

by maintaining the part of you that is unoccupied.

~ Lao Tzu,
The Complete Works of Lao Tzu: Tao Teh Ching & Hua Hu Ching

Introduction: Embracing Your Personal Power

What does it really mean to step fully into your personal power, or to embrace it? The underlying concept of stepping into personal power is the same for all of us, but the nature of your life and your life mission may be quite different than mine or any other person's in the world. While I am led to write and teach about love and compassion, you may be led to excel as an artist, to create art of the same magnitude as Michelangelo. Perhaps your life mission is to be a superstar athlete, win 10 Olympic gold medals, and go on to mentor emerging young superstars from around the world. Maybe you have a religious calling and want to pastor a church, teaching and tending compassionately to your flock. If you are handicapped, your life mission might be to accept your condition, live a joy-filled life, becoming an example of compassion and forgiveness to those who care for you. If you are a farmer, your life mission might be to successfully supply your country with healthy, organic fresh fruit and vegetables. If you are an adolescent suffering from an undiagnosed illness, your mission might be to teach your medical team to think outside the box, later writing about your experience, touching the lives of millions of people. There are as many life missions as there are people. We are all unique. We are all important.

To step fully into your personal power, it is necessary to put away your fear and worry. It is necessary to accept yourself exactly as you were yesterday and exactly as you are today. As you do that, you can accept the person you will become tomorrow without fear. Life is a process and there is not one thing you can do to disturb your process, rush it, or change it. This does not mean you are powerless. It means that you are very, very powerful. I look back at my life and know that I had to live those early experiences in order to become the person I am today. I had to live each day and each event just as it occurred. Some days were devastating and almost impossible to endure. Much of my early life was emotionally and physically terrifying. Did I have enough love and support to keep me moving forward? Yes, there was always someone who loved me enough to point me in the right direction. At one time I believed I had no one to guide me and teach me. My pain blocked my view of reality. I had many magnificent people who touched my life, and their caring helped keep my inner spark alive. You have at least one magnificent person who has loved and mentored you.

Each of us has a spiritual family that loves us, guides us, and teaches us. Today I am lucky enough to know my spiritual family by name and have a personal relationship with each of them. Like all families, the relationship with each individual member is different. I love and accept each of them and the roles they play in my life. The time I spend with each shifts depending on what I need in order to strengthen my journey. I discover something new every day, and I am always excited to learn. I may have spiritual family members I have not yet met, but that is OK. Each of us has human family members that we'll never meet, but they are there, and they energetically influence our life. Even the unknown is important to our journey.

What are the personal emotional–spiritual characteristics I learn from my spiritual family members: the virtues and personal characteristics they exhibit as they interact with me? They are loving, forgiving, compassionate educators. They accept me as I am and love me whether I am successful or not. They are there for me in every life situation. They travel with me, go to the grocery store with me, go on vacation with me, go to work with me, go to the doctor with me, and sit beside my bed when I have the flu. They were there when my children were born and walked with me through each childhood mishap, each pleasure, and each milestone as my children grew into adults. They are helping me right now as I write, guiding each word and actually putting the next thought into my mind.

How does my spiritual family do all they do for me and never get frustrated, angry, or disappointed with me? They live each moment as if they were in active meditation. They are calm, peaceful, gentle, relaxed, clear of thought, focused, reality-based, honest, compassionate, forgiving, joyful, and always quick with a joke. They maintain their presence because they have attained absolute mindfulness and live each moment filled with the energy of love. Their energy field is pure love, which means they are safe, trusting, and fearless. Their tremendous power comes to them because their minds are quiet, still, and receptive. They are 100% connected to the wisdom, power, and guidance of Creation. They know exactly who they are, they know they are limitless in their ability, they know my potential is limitless; I know your potential is the same as mine.

So, what do I need to do to step fully into my potential? I accept my life as it has been up to this second. I realize that I have been given exactly what I needed in order to fulfill my life mission. I continue to adopt the life skills that my spiritual family teaches me through the examples of their lives. I attempt to live life in exactly the same loving, kind way they live their lives. That means I choose to live each moment as if I were in active mediation, giving myself the feelings of peace and safety within, filling my energy field with the love of Creation, and working to fulfill my life mission by doing the writing and teaching that I am meant to do.

We are constantly being given messages from our spiritual family. We don't always recognize them as messages and many of us doubt the sanity of those who talk about their spiritual life in the way I am about to share with you. The following stories are examples of how spiritual communication can and does occur. Sometimes it is through sound or smell. Sometimes it is through a symbol that has special meaning to you; sometimes it is through repeating numbers, a message on a license plate, or a butterfly landing on your arm. After my client's brother died at a very young age, she was distraught. She told me how she sat crying, worrying about him, praying for him. Then a beautiful butterfly came to her and landed on her shoulder and sat there for a second. She said she felt her brother's presence and knew he was OK. The butterfly brought her peace of mind.

This morning I woke up at exactly 1:56 a.m. I remember because I awakened suddenly and looked at the clock. I've learned to respect occurrences that are sudden and outside my normal range of experience as they always alert me to an incoming spiritual communication. One of the first communication signals I recognized as such was a loud, sharp buzzing in my right ear that would either begin as I was about to fall asleep or awaken me during the night. Intuition told me the buzzing was a 'spiritual doorbell' and I needed to pay attention. Once recognized as a request for my attention, I began to receive a series of profound life-changing messages from one of my spiritual family members. The buzzing rarely happens now, but communication has not stopped. Currently my family seems to enjoy showing me numbers and directing me to people who have spent years learning the significance of these numbers. There are two sites on the internet that I believe to be valid and heavily researched. One is created by Dr. Doreen Virtue. I made note to check her Angel Numbers because I knew they would help me understand the early morning awakening. The numbers were a reminder that my life is changing drastically and an encouragement to trust and open my mind and heart to other changes that are also coming about. If numbers are constantly appearing in your life and you are curious about them you can check http://spiritlibrary.com/doreen-virtue/angel-numbers, or Dr. Virtue's book *Healing with the Angels* (1999).

When I went back to sleep, I began to have an instructional dream that introduced concepts my spiritual family wanted me to embrace more fully. I had images of one tree after another, and I recognized each of them as representing the Tree of Life. I saw a tree, it disappeared, and the next tree appeared. Then I saw them all lined up, and sensed that each tree represented one day in my life. The trees looked like perfectly shaped apple trees on an art deco post card, but the apples on my trees were words written on white cards attached to the branches. The first tree had a mixture of words like love, compassion, sadness, grief, trust, safety, forgiveness, joy. The second tree had a similar mixture of words: love, life, power, trust, pain, change, joy, care, compassion, receive. Then a third tree with some very high-frequency words and others words representing painful human experiences. The trees kept coming; each with a different set of words, but each had the same mix of negative and positive words. This went on for what seemed like hours, and I asked my spiritual teachers to explain the lesson. They said, "Do you think anyone's life is pain free? Do you think that a tree has a painless life? Do you think a rabbit living in the woods has a painless life?" They inferred that their lives were not without difficulties. I understood what they were teaching. Each day is a mixture of all kinds of experiences and opportunities offering me a wide range of emotional options. It is up to me to live a mindful life: Accept the good with the bad; learn from the good and the bad. Life is for learning and always contains a wide range of experiences. We can choose to be overwhelmed by experiences, or we can learn to accept the teachings and move forward with love, faith, and trust in Creation. Every experience, regardless of how painful it might be, brings a gift.

When morning came, I rested and thought about my instructional experience; the 1:56 notification that a communication was coming and then the dream itself. I decided to meditate using my usual pattern, and when I finally got up it was 7:12 a.m. I was told to go directly to my computer and write. It is now 10:03 a.m. I feel great, am not hungry, and I have not yet eaten my breakfast or taken my morning nutritional supplements. This morning's messages were spiritual reinforcement, not much different than a mom reminding her child to remember his or her lunch and make sure their homework assignments are in their backpack. Today I have been reminded I can trust the changes that are occurring. The dream presenting the days of my life let me know that my emotions are normal and reminded me that I have a choice to embrace them or be overwhelmed by them. I am to continue to learn and share and I am to "take nothing for granted, and always stay as relaxed and conscious as I can so I am able to receive the information my spiritual family wants me to have."

How does all of this apply to your Nurturing Wellness Through Radical Self-Care journey? That is for you to decide, because the messages above will be interpreted by each reader and applied to each life in a unique way. Each of us needs love, help, and support. This program offers support as a very detailed outline of one of the paths you can take to achieve a richer, fuller life. The program presents flexible structure that, within the guidelines of the program, gives you the ability to take what you need and leave the rest. You have the opportunity to learn how to build a mindful lifestyle. You are given examples of guided mindfulness meditation. You have the opportunity to learn a very easy way of keeping your autonomic nervous system balanced and functioning so that it's fluid and efficient. You have an opportunity to combine energy psychology with mindfulness, journaling, and life-giving affirmations. I hope you take what you need and change your life for the better.

Dedicate each day to living relaxed and worry-free. Consciously open your heart to the flow of Creation and Creation's energy. By doing so, you have the power to create each day, one day at a time.

CHAPTER 6

Daily Release Work (Easy Access Directions)

Your work can be gentle using passive release, or your work can be active, using the REB emotional release technique. Passive release happens by setting a desired outcome, noticing your thoughts and body sensations, breathing, and resting in the posture. Active release happens when you use bilateral squeezing or swaying. The directions below use bilateral squeezing or swaying. If you want a softer session, omit the squeezing and swaying. A typical release session without meditation lasts 10–15 minutes.

Have your workbook and a pen or pencil with you as you begin your daily release work. Notice what you are feeling and thinking. Make a note of it in these pre-session sections of your **Nurturing Wellness Journal Page**:

- Desired Outcome
- My Mood Today
- Gratitude for Today
- Affirmations you'll be using today

Some people like to meditate before they do their daily work, feeling it creates better success. If you are one of them, listen to your meditation now.

- ➤ Decide if you are going to work with passive release or active release. Work at a comfortable speed, giving yourself time to process the work you are doing.
- ➤ Engage the REB Relaxation Posture and begin to relax. Remember to place your tongue on the gum ridge behind your upper teeth. Breathe from your abdomen and through your nose. Take all the time you need.
- ➤ Notice when the relaxation begins to soothe your body. Once you feel the relaxation, begin the bilateral squeezing or swaying.
- ➤ While engaged in the release work, read the first affirmation on your list. Pause after reading it. Remain in the posture. Take a naturally deep breath. Read the affirmation a second time. Pause, and take a naturally deep breath.
- ➤ Mindfully listen to what your mind–body–spirit has to say about the affirmation you have just worked with. Notice what you are thinking and feeling emotionally and physically.
- ➤ Ask yourself, "What is different?" Notice as much about the process as you can. The more you notice the better. You are a witness to the process.
- ➤ If you have a strong emotional response to one or more of the affirmations, use the section below from the **Nurturing Wellness Journal Page** to help guide you through the release of feelings.

SUDS: Subjective Units of Distress
Rate your distress on a scale between 0 (low) and 10 (high). Aim to achieve an ending SUDS of 2 or below.

Beginning **SUDS** level _____   Ending **SUDS** level _____

* Fill out "After the session I noticed _____" section on your **Nurturing Wellness Journal Page** and complete the page.

Repeat the steps above for each affirmation on your list, using the SUDS work only for the one affirmation that challenged you most.

> ➤ When all work is completed, fill out the "I noticed that my daily sessions are creating positive changes" portion of the sheet.
> ➤ Many people have a lot to say after their session. Write down anything you want to remember. Insights don't stay with you, even though you think they will. Use **This Week's Insights** pages for your weekly logs.
> ➤ Use a **Heart Massage** as a way to say, "thank you" to *you* for doing the work today. Say, "thank you" to your mind and body for working in harmony with you. Say, "thank you" for whatever is in your heart.

Systems Theory

My family works like a system
Each family member has a job, a role to play.

I live daily within a community of systems.
Education, economic, medical ...

My country engages other countries in a multitude of man-made systems.
Banking, trade, military alliances ...

Earth is one planet within a solar system of planets.
Our solar system is one within a universe of solar systems.

There is a feeling of perpetual movement, perpetual cooperation.
To survive, our planet needs our solar system and our universe.

All varieties of life on Earth depend upon the existence of our planet.
All life is interdependent, one life form needing another life form to survive.

There is a delicate balance that keeps us all flowing in just the right way.
Balance is required to preserve the chain of life, to preserve Earth.

Our body is healthy only when balance is maintained.
Our mind and emotions are healthy only when balance is maintained.

Many humans are out of balance, struggling to survive.
The Earth struggles for balance.

All must learn to cooperate, compromise, offer kindness, compassion ... become functional systems.
If you and I just love, all will remain; Life will continue, if you and I just love.

~ *Janet Gallagher Nestor*

The Nurturing Wellness Affirmations

The affirmations are your starting point. With them, combined with Radiant Energies Balance, you begin to release your stress and anxiety and their underlying cause. Think of each affirmation as a suggestion for positive thought—the beginning of a whole new life where more and more of your thoughts and beliefs are positive. Right now you might be saying, "My thoughts and beliefs are positive! I've always been a positive person." There is research that says the odds are you are not as positive as you believe yourself to be. Some research shows the average person's thoughts are as much as 60% to 85% negative, or 15% to 40% positive! Whether this is true for you or not, my next statement is very important. It takes three positive thoughts to negate the impact of one negative thought. People who actually thrive in their lives have far more positive thoughts than three to one!

There is a whole new field in psychology called Positive Psychology. You might want to take a look at the following website, read the research on positive thought, and determine for yourself the importance of a positive, mindful life. The Positivity Ratio mentioned above was developed by Dr. Barbara Fredrickson, University of North Carolina (http://www.unc.edu/peplab/barb_fredrickson_page.html). While you're browsing through the information, take her Positivity Test and check your Positivity.

Create a positive life, one day at a time.

Readiness

- I am worthy of good health and well-being.
- I accept myself as I am today, with all of my strengths and all of my shortcomings.
- I deserve to be over my problems.
- I am willing to be over my problems.
- I have a right to be alive.
- I celebrate my life.
- I am safe and healing is safe for me.
- Others are safe if I get over my problems.
- I work through my problems with love, self-compassion, and confidence.
- My relationship with life is positive.
- I am content to allow my life to unfold one day at a time.
- I welcome positive change at all levels of my being.
- My heart is filled with love and joy.
- I forgive and release all the issues and perceptions that have sabotaged my efforts toward health and positive well-being.
- I am working this program the best way I know how.
- I am a worthy person.

Positive Core Beliefs and General Well-Being

- I am balanced, centered, happy, and healthy.
- My thoughts are clear, positive, and supportive.
- I am insightful, competent, and confident in my abilities.
- I am loving and lovable.
- I joyfully embrace my creativity.
- I fully and joyfully embrace my personal power.
- I am a powerful person.
- I view each life event as an opportunity for increased self-awareness.
- I allow myself to play, laugh, and have fun.
- I recognize that play, laughter, and fun are essential to my overall well-being.
- Each part of my life is balanced with my need to rest and rejuvenate.
- I am free to make all of my own choices.
- I am a whole person, and I claim my potential.

Self-Care

- I intentionally create a comfortable and cozy living space for myself.
- My living space is filled with things I love, and things that make me happy.
- I wear clothes with colors that make me happy.
- I live within, or visit regularly, the physical environment that feeds my soul.
- I am mentally–emotionally–spiritually nurtured when I am _____ (choose the environment that fills you up and brings you inner joy).
  Examples: by the ocean, in the mountains, in the hustle and bustle of the city, on a farm, in the forest.
- I surround myself with people who love and respect me.
- I care for myself realistically, with understanding and compassion.
- When the situation is warranted, I can say, "yes" (or "no") with clarity and confidence.
- I maintain a schedule that allows me quiet time and enough rest and sleep.
- I care for my mental, emotional, spiritual, and physical needs every day.
- I honor and welcome all positive emotions into my heart and soul.
- I seek medical and mental health services when I am in need of care.

Body Image and Body Awareness

- I honor my body as my home.
- I feel safe in my body.
- I honor my body's capacity for strength and wellness.
- I believe in my body's ability to achieve and maintain its highest level of wellness.
- My cells, my organs, and my immune system are strong.
- I am grateful to my body for supporting my life.
- I know that my life story began at my conception (or birth), and I write the plot and choose the characters.
- I take time to listen to my body, and I respond with heightened awareness.
- I acknowledge and honor my multi-sensory communication system: sight, hearing, touch, taste, smell, intuition, and my ability to communicate non-verbally.
- I honor my body's automatic life-support systems: my nervous system, my heartbeat, the expanding and contracting of my lungs, the circulation of my blood, the digestion of food, the miracle of my immune system.
- I honor my body's ability for natural and beautiful movement: walking, playing, dancing, running, and jumping.
- I welcome and honor my femininity (or masculinity) and my sexual energy.
- My body–mind–spirit and emotions are positive and interactive.
- I welcome a positive, insightful relationship with my body.

My Relationship with Food

Choose only the affirmations that apply to you. I recommend you include the safety affirmations when you choose any of the affirmations from this list.

- My relationship with food is enjoyable and empowering.
- I eat and enjoy healthy foods.
- When hungry, I satisfy my hunger with healthy foods.
- I honor all the systems of my body with positive nutritional choices.
- I recognize emotional hunger (*emotional need to restrict, need to eat compulsively, need to binge, need to purge*) when it occurs, and I release all the associated troubling emotions in all layers of my being.
- I recognize the emotional need to exercise compulsively when it occurs and I release all the associated troubling emotions in all layers of my being.
- I feel safe in my relationship with food and the relationship is positive.
- I feel safe in the world and my relationship with food is positive.
- I embrace and meet my emotional needs and maintain a positive relationship with food.
- I rely on my peaceful inner nature and my relationship with food is constant, positive, and healthy.
- Food supports the functions of my body.
- Self-care, including healthy eating, supports my emotional–spiritual health.

Self-Esteem

- My positive thoughts are my friends, and they guide me well.
- I accept who I was yesterday and who I am today.
- I am an amazing person with much to offer.
- I am fully alive and glad to be here.
- I am a loving and lovable person.
- My opinion matters.
- I have compassion for myself and others.
- I am loved, cared about, and wanted.
- I am powerless over you and your thoughts, actions, and behavior.
- I accept anger as a normal human emotion.
- I accept all of my emotions for what they are today.
- My inner nature is wise and peaceful.
- Self-care, including healthy eating, supports my emotional–spiritual health.
- I feel safe in the world and safe with myself.
- As I strengthen my body with gentle exercise, I strengthen my mind and my self-confidence.
- I am growing in self-awareness, self-understanding, and self-worth.
- I have choices, and I am free to make decisions that guide my life.

Worry, Anxiety, Fear, Obsessive Thoughts, and Addictive Behaviors

- I am safe.
- I am safe when I connect with my heart's emotions.
- I am worthy of living a full and joyous life.
- I am loved and wanted.
- I am wonderful just the way I am.
- I release the emotions and issues of each day and leave tomorrow to tomorrow.
- I am at peace with my emotions.
- I digest my emotions and the issues of my life with ease.
- I release the past with joy.
- I choose to live my life with zest and joy.
- I allow the process of life to flow around and through me.
- I am the author of my own life.
- I live my life with a positive, now-oriented focus.
- Life is a journey, and I have plenty of time.
- I attract positive people and opportunities.
- I approve of who I am today and who I am becoming.
- My goals are realistic and achievable.

Sadness, Grief, and Loss

- I have the capacity to feel happy and whole.
- I love and accept myself as I am today.
- I acknowledge and accept my sadness (or grief, loss).
- In my circumstances, sadness and grief are normal feelings, and I allow myself to fully experience them.
- I care for myself and all my basic needs.
- I accept love and compassion from my family and friends.
- I tell my family and friends what I need and accept their offerings of love and kindness.
- I ask for help, support, and comfort when I need it.
- I stay active and value each moment.
- I trust Universal Wisdom (God, Higher Power, myself, my family) and therefore feel safe.
- I am willing to let go and let God.
- I choose love for myself and for others.
- Even with the sadness and grief, I feel the spark of light and love within.
- I am open to new experiences and new ways of being.
- I trust my inner wisdom to guide and support my deepest needs.
- I welcome each new day with hope and a positive heart.

Anger

- Anger is a human emotion and is neither negative nor positive until I categorize it.
- I realize that anger is my body's emotional signal to stop, look, and listen.
- I give myself permission to feel relaxed and peaceful.
- No one has the power to make me angry.
- An individual who has the power to anger me has the power to control me.
- Anger comes from within me, and I am responsible for my feelings.
- Anger has a lot of power that can be channeled into positive action.
- Anger has the power to motivate me toward positive change.
- I forgive myself for allowing my anger to control me.
- I have the ability to calm and soothe myself.
- I have the ability to let go of my frustrations.
- I have the ability to let go of my resentments.
- I have the ability to forgive myself for my mistakes.
- I have the ability to feel compassion for others.
- I choose to let go of my need to "get even."
- Deep, gentle breathing has the ability to calm and soothe me.
- I no longer have to keep my anger buried deep within.
- I have permission to express my anger and the power to create positive change.

Trust

- As I release the past, I embrace today with a trusting attitude.
- When I trust, joy is present in my life.
- I trust myself to make wise choices.
- I trust that I am strong enough and loving enough to heal and grow.
- I trust the Universe to bring the right people and opportunities into my life.
- I trust my feelings.
- When I need to know something, I trust myself to ask the right questions.
- I trust the power of unconditional love to heal and guide me.
- I trust that my inner nature is wise.
- I trust myself to handle each new life development with wisdom and grace.
- I am thankful for all my opportunities to learn, even the ones that are uncomfortable for me.
- I trust the people and professionals I have chosen for my support network.
- The more I let go of my need to control, the more powerful I am.
- The more I let go and trust, the more powerful I become.
- The more I let go and trust, the healthier I become.
- The more I let go and trust, the more alive I become.
- I trust myself in every way.

Forgiveness

- Acceptance is the first step toward forgiveness.
- Compassion for self and others enhances my ability to forgive.
- With love and compassion, I forgive the imperfections in myself and others.
- I forgive myself for believing that my family's mistakes are my mistakes.
- I accept my life as it has been up to this moment.
- I am free to be who I am today.
- Even though I am imperfect, I am free to love myself and others.
- I give myself permission to be free, happy, and lighthearted.
- I am free and able to smile, laugh, and play.
- I accept my personal value and worth.
- I become stronger and wiser each time I let go and forgive.
- My personal power expands as I gain in my ability to love compassionately.
- My self-trust is directly related to my ability to forgive myself and others.
- I unlock the door to the peacefulness and joy that lives within.
- I am safe if I let go and forgive.
- Others are safe if I let go and forgive.
- I am worthy of giving and receiving unconditional love.

Boosting My Immune System

- Love heals me.
- With each inhale, I breathe love into my body.
- Love is my connection to inner wisdom and universal consciousness.
- Health and strength fill my body all day long.
- I love my body.
- I have a nurturing and supportive community of loved ones around me.
- I remain positive and hopeful.
- I eat healthy foods my body likes and is able to digest easily.
- I live one day at a time with gratitude.
- I live each day with clarity and confidence.
- I travel lightly through life and release all unwanted negative emotional baggage.
- I choose to enjoy my life: To love sing, play, laugh, create.
- I live free of fear, one day at a time.
- I honor the rejuvenation needs of my body with comforting rest and sleep.
- My healing comes as a result of deep internal restfulness.
- My body is hydrated with good, clean, fresh water.
- I choose to nurture myself with positive thoughts, words, and actions.
- I nurture my relationships with the unconditional love of Creation.
- I feel safe in the world I have created for myself.

CHAPTER 7

My Friend

. . . .

Work hard my Friend—your heart is weary,
Your mind full of fear and failure.
Fear is not an issue here; For one can only succeed.
Deep within your being there is Creation's Love
And where there is Creation Love, success is your reality.

~ *Anonymous*

Workbook Pages

Week 1: Love Yourself

In one day, one hour, everything could be arranged at once! The chief thing is to love.
~ Fyodor Dostoyevsky

Program: Choose Daily Meditation or Readiness Affirmations
If working with Readiness Affirmations, create your list below:

This Week's Insights

This page will appear each week. Use it to make notes from your daily work, jotting down important self-awareness information, ideas, and insights you want to remember.

Self-Care First!

Positive emotional and physical self-care is the most beautiful gift that you can give to yourself and your family. Put a check beside the activity on the days you engage in it. Meditation, at least once each week, is part of the Nurturing Wellness Through Radical Self-Care Program. The other listed activities are optional. Yoga and Tai Chi are good for energy flow. Yoga is great for depression and Tai Chi is great support for trauma survivors. Consider making one or both of them part of your rejuvenation program.

Meditation: _____ _____ _____ _____ _____ _____ _____

Meditation Journal: _____ _____ _____ _____ _____ _____ _____

Walking Meditation: _____ _____ _____ _____ _____ _____ _____

Breathing Meditation: _____ _____ _____ _____ _____ _____ _____

Exercise Walk: _____ _____ _____ _____ _____ _____ _____

Yoga: _____ _____ _____ _____ _____ _____ _____

Tai Chi: _____ _____ _____ _____ _____ _____ _____

Bubble Bath / Hot Tub: _____ _____ _____ _____ _____ _____ _____

Gym Workout: _____ _____ _____ _____ _____ _____ _____

Running or Jogging: _____ _____ _____ _____ _____ _____ _____

Team or Partner Sports: _____ _____ _____ _____ _____ _____ _____

Swimming: _____ _____ _____ _____ _____ _____ _____

Aerobics Class: _____ _____ _____ _____ _____ _____ _____

Massage and Body Work / Energy Healing: _____ _____ _____ _____ _____ _____ _____

Manicure or Pedicure: _____

Other: (List the activity or exercise below):

_____ : _____ _____ _____ _____ _____ _____ _____

_____ : _____ _____ _____ _____ _____ _____ _____

_____ : _____ _____ _____ _____ _____ _____ _____

Nurturing Wellness Journal Page

Day # _____ Desired Outcome _____

My Mood today is (check all that apply):

Good _____	Flat (Blah) _____	Depressed _____	Very depressed _____
Content _____	Erratic _____	Slightly Manic _____	Highly Manic _____
Angry _____	Anxious/fearful _____	Joyful _____	Hopeful _____

I woke up feeling rested today _____

Gratitude for today _____

I noticed the following emotions, body sensations, and thoughts *before* the session (list below):

Affirmation Group (if choosing a group): _____

After the session I noticed (place an X beside each YES answer):

_____ I was relaxed   _____ I felt positive about my experience

_____ I was agitated / anxious   _____ One or more of the affirmations challenged me

(Optional) Each day you have the option to choose one affirmation from your list for in-depth work.
Affirmation _____

SUDS: Subjective Units of Distress
Rate your distress on a scale between 0 (low) and 10 (high). Aim to achieve an ending SUDS of 2 or below.

Beginning **SUDS** level _____   Ending **SUDS** level _____

I notice that my daily sessions are creating positive changes (place an X beside each YES answer):

_____ in my relationship with others   _____ in my relationship with myself

_____ in my self-care program   _____ in my perception of my health / wellness

_____ in my ability to work through challenging issues and emotions

_____ in my confidence level and my feelings of self-worth

_____ in my daily activity level   _____ in my perception of personal safety

_____ in my level of inner awareness   _____ in my attitude toward life and its possibilities

_____ in my level of ability to grow and change

Other change _____

_____ Heart Massage

Nurturing Wellness Journal Page

Day # _____ **Desired Outcome** _____

My Mood today is (check all that apply):

Good	_____	Flat (Blah)	_____	Depressed	_____	Very depressed	_____
Content	_____	Erratic	_____	Slightly Manic	_____	Highly Manic	_____
Angry	_____	Anxious/fearful	_____	Joyful	_____	Hopeful	_____

I woke up feeling rested today _____

Gratitude for today _____

I noticed the following emotions, body sensations, and thoughts *before* the session (list below):

Affirmation Group (if choosing a group): _____

After the session I noticed (place an X beside each YES answer):

_____ I was relaxed   _____ I felt positive about my experience

_____ I was agitated / anxious   _____ One or more of the affirmations challenged me

(Optional) Each day you have the option to choose one affirmation from your list for in-depth work. Affirmation _____

SUDS: Subjective Units of Distress
Rate your distress on a scale between 0 (low) and 10 (high). Aim to achieve an ending SUDS of 2 or below.

Beginning **SUDS** level _____   Ending **SUDS** level _____

I notice that my daily sessions are creating positive changes (place an X beside each YES answer):

_____ in my relationship with others   _____ in my relationship with myself

_____ in my self-care program   _____ in my perception of my health / wellness

_____ in my ability to work through challenging issues and emotions

_____ in my confidence level and my feelings of self-worth

_____ in my daily activity level   _____ in my perception of personal safety

_____ in my level of inner awareness   _____ in my attitude toward life and its possibilities

_____ in my level of ability to grow and change

Other change _____

_____ Heart Massage

Nurturing Wellness Journal Page

Day # _____ **Desired Outcome** _____

My Mood today is (check all that apply):

Good _____	Flat (Blah) _____	Depressed _____	Very depressed _____
Content _____	Erratic _____	Slightly Manic _____	Highly Manic _____
Angry _____	Anxious/fearful _____	Joyful _____	Hopeful _____

I woke up feeling rested today _____

Gratitude for today _____

I noticed the following emotions, body sensations, and thoughts *before* **the session** (list below):

Affirmation Group (if choosing a group): _____

After the session I noticed (place an X beside each YES answer):

_____ I was relaxed   _____ I felt positive about my experience

_____ I was agitated / anxious   _____ One or more of the affirmations challenged me

(Optional) Each day you have the option to choose one affirmation from your list for in-depth work.
Affirmation _____

SUDS: Subjective Units of Distress
Rate your distress on a scale between 0 (low) and 10 (high). Aim to achieve an ending SUDS of 2 or below.

Beginning **SUDS** level _____   Ending **SUDS** level _____

I notice that my daily sessions are creating positive changes (place an X beside each YES answer):

_____ in my relationship with others   _____ in my relationship with myself

_____ in my self-care program   _____ in my perception of my health / wellness

_____ in my ability to work through challenging issues and emotions

_____ in my confidence level and my feelings of self-worth

_____ in my daily activity level   _____ in my perception of personal safety

_____ in my level of inner awareness   _____ in my attitude toward life and its possibilities

_____ in my level of ability to grow and change

Other change _____

_____ Heart Massage

Nurturing Wellness Journal Page

Day # _____ **Desired Outcome** _____

My Mood today is (check all that apply):

Good _____	Flat (Blah) _____	Depressed _____	Very depressed _____
Content _____	Erratic _____	Slightly Manic _____	Highly Manic _____
Angry _____	Anxious/fearful _____	Joyful _____	Hopeful _____

I woke up feeling rested today _____

Gratitude for today _____

I noticed the following emotions, body sensations, and thoughts *before* the session (list below):

Affirmation Group (if choosing a group): _____

After the session I noticed (place an X beside each YES answer):

_____ I was relaxed   _____ I felt positive about my experience

_____ I was agitated / anxious   _____ One or more of the affirmations challenged me

(Optional) Each day you have the option to choose one affirmation from your list for in-depth work.
Affirmation _____

SUDS: Subjective Units of Distress
Rate your distress on a scale between 0 (low) and 10 (high). Aim to achieve an ending SUDS of 2 or below.

Beginning **SUDS** level _____   Ending **SUDS** level _____

I notice that my daily sessions are creating positive changes (place an X beside each YES answer):

_____ in my relationship with others   _____ in my relationship with myself

_____ in my self-care program   _____ in my perception of my health / wellness

_____ in my ability to work through challenging issues and emotions

_____ in my confidence level and my feelings of self-worth

_____ in my daily activity level   _____ in my perception of personal safety

_____ in my level of inner awareness   _____ in my attitude toward life and its possibilities

_____ in my level of ability to grow and change

Other change _____

_____ Heart Massage

Nurturing Wellness Journal Page

Day # _____   Desired Outcome _____

My Mood today is (check all that apply):

Good _____	Flat (Blah) _____	Depressed _____	Very depressed _____
Content _____	Erratic _____	Slightly Manic _____	Highly Manic _____
Angry _____	Anxious/fearful _____	Joyful _____	Hopeful _____

I woke up feeling rested today _____

Gratitude for today _____

I noticed the following emotions, body sensations, and thoughts *before* the session (list below):

Affirmation Group (if choosing a group): _____

After the session I noticed (place an X beside each YES answer):

_____ I was relaxed   _____ I felt positive about my experience

_____ I was agitated / anxious   _____ One or more of the affirmations challenged me

(Optional) Each day you have the option to choose one affirmation from your list for in-depth work.
Affirmation _____

SUDS: Subjective Units of Distress
Rate your distress on a scale between 0 (low) and 10 (high). Aim to achieve an ending SUDS of 2 or below.

Beginning **SUDS** level _____   Ending **SUDS** level _____

I notice that my daily sessions are creating positive changes (place an X beside each YES answer):

_____ in my relationship with others   _____ in my relationship with myself

_____ in my self-care program   _____ in my perception of my health / wellness

_____ in my ability to work through challenging issues and emotions

_____ in my confidence level and my feelings of self-worth

_____ in my daily activity level   _____ in my perception of personal safety

_____ in my level of inner awareness   _____ in my attitude toward life and its possibilities

_____ in my level of ability to grow and change

Other change _____

_____ Heart Massage

Week 2: Know Yourself

By understanding the self, all this universe is known.
~ The Upanishads

Program: Meditations, Readiness Affirmations, or Begin Affirmation List Work
If working with Affirmations, create your weekly list below:

This Week's Insights

When people believe in themselves, they have the first secret to success.
~ Norman Vincent Peale

Self-Care First!

Positive emotional and physical self-care is the most beautiful gift that you can give to yourself and your family. Put a check beside the activity on the days you engage in it. Meditation, at least once each week, is part of the Nurturing Wellness Through Radical Self-Care Program. The other listed activities are optional. Yoga and Tai Chi are good for energy flow. Yoga is great for depression and Tai Chi is great support for trauma survivors. Consider making one or both of them part of your rejuvenation program.

Meditation: _____ _____ _____ _____ _____ _____ _____

Meditation Journal: _____ _____ _____ _____ _____ _____ _____

Walking Meditation: _____ _____ _____ _____ _____ _____ _____

Breathing Meditation: _____ _____ _____ _____ _____ _____ _____

Exercise Walk: _____ _____ _____ _____ _____ _____ _____

Yoga: _____ _____ _____ _____ _____ _____ _____

Tai Chi: _____ _____ _____ _____ _____ _____ _____

Bubble Bath / Hot Tub: _____ _____ _____ _____ _____ _____ _____

Gym Workout: _____ _____ _____ _____ _____ _____ _____

Running or Jogging: _____ _____ _____ _____ _____ _____ _____

Team or Partner Sports: _____ _____ _____ _____ _____ _____ _____

Swimming: _____ _____ _____ _____ _____ _____ _____

Aerobics Class: _____ _____ _____ _____ _____ _____ _____

Massage and Body Work / Energy Healing: _____ _____ _____ _____ _____ _____ _____

Manicure or Pedicure: _____

Other: (List the activity or exercise below):

_____: _____ _____ _____ _____ _____ _____ _____

_____: _____ _____ _____ _____ _____ _____ _____

_____: _____ _____ _____ _____ _____ _____ _____

Nurturing Wellness Journal Page

Day # _____ **Desired Outcome** _____

My Mood today is (check all that apply):

Good _____	Flat (Blah) _____	Depressed _____	Very depressed _____
Content _____	Erratic _____	Slightly Manic _____	Highly Manic _____
Angry _____	Anxious/fearful _____	Joyful _____	Hopeful _____

I woke up feeling rested today _____

Gratitude for today _____

I noticed the following emotions, body sensations, and thoughts *before* **the session** (list below):

Affirmation Group (if choosing a group): _____

After the session I noticed (place an X beside each YES answer):

_____ I was relaxed   _____ I felt positive about my experience

_____ I was agitated / anxious   _____ One or more of the affirmations challenged me

(Optional) Each day you have the option to choose one affirmation from your list for in-depth work.
Affirmation _____

SUDS: Subjective Units of Distress
Rate your distress on a scale between 0 (low) and 10 (high). Aim to achieve an ending SUDS of 2 or below.

Beginning **SUDS** level _____   Ending **SUDS** level _____

I notice that my daily sessions are creating positive changes (place an X beside each YES answer):

_____ in my relationship with others   _____ in my relationship with myself
_____ in my self-care program   _____ in my perception of my health / wellness
_____ in my ability to work through challenging issues and emotions
_____ in my confidence level and my feelings of self-worth
_____ in my daily activity level   _____ in my perception of personal safety
_____ in my level of inner awareness   _____ in my attitude toward life and its possibilities
_____ in my level of ability to grow and change

Other change _____

_____ Heart Massage

Nurturing Wellness Journal Page

Day # _____ **Desired Outcome** _____

My Mood today is (check all that apply):

Good _____	Flat (Blah) _____	Depressed _____	Very depressed _____
Content _____	Erratic _____	Slightly Manic _____	Highly Manic _____
Angry _____	Anxious/fearful _____	Joyful _____	Hopeful _____

I woke up feeling rested today _____

Gratitude for today _____

I noticed the following emotions, body sensations, and thoughts *before* **the session** (list below):

Affirmation Group (if choosing a group): _____

After the session I noticed (place an X beside each YES answer):

_____ I was relaxed   _____ I felt positive about my experience

_____ I was agitated / anxious   _____ One or more of the affirmations challenged me

(Optional) Each day you have the option to choose one affirmation from your list for in-depth work.
Affirmation _____

SUDS: Subjective Units of Distress
Rate your distress on a scale between 0 (low) and 10 (high). Aim to achieve an ending SUDS of 2 or below.

Beginning **SUDS** level _____   Ending **SUDS** level _____

I notice that my daily sessions are creating positive changes (place an X beside each YES answer):

_____ in my relationship with others   _____ in my relationship with myself

_____ in my self-care program   _____ in my perception of my health / wellness

_____ in my ability to work through challenging issues and emotions

_____ in my confidence level and my feelings of self-worth

_____ in my daily activity level   _____ in my perception of personal safety

_____ in my level of inner awareness   _____ in my attitude toward life and its possibilities

_____ in my level of ability to grow and change

Other change _____

_____ Heart Massage

Nurturing Wellness Journal Page

Day # _____   Desired Outcome _____

My Mood today is (check all that apply):

Good _____	Flat (Blah) _____	Depressed _____	Very depressed _____
Content _____	Erratic _____	Slightly Manic _____	Highly Manic _____
Angry _____	Anxious/fearful _____	Joyful _____	Hopeful _____

I woke up feeling rested today   _____

Gratitude for today _____

I noticed the following emotions, body sensations, and thoughts *before* **the session** (list below):

Affirmation Group (if choosing a group): _____

After the session I noticed (place an X beside each YES answer):

_____ I was relaxed   _____ I felt positive about my experience

_____ I was agitated / anxious   _____ One or more of the affirmations challenged me

(Optional) Each day you have the option to choose one affirmation from your list for in-depth work.
Affirmation _____

SUDS: Subjective Units of Distress
Rate your distress on a scale between 0 (low) and 10 (high). Aim to achieve an ending SUDS of 2 or below.

Beginning **SUDS** level _____   Ending **SUDS** level _____

I notice that my daily sessions are creating positive changes (place an X beside each YES answer):

_____ in my relationship with others   _____ in my relationship with myself

_____ in my self-care program   _____ in my perception of my health / wellness

_____ in my ability to work through challenging issues and emotions

_____ in my confidence level and my feelings of self-worth

_____ in my daily activity level   _____ in my perception of personal safety

_____ in my level of inner awareness   _____ in my attitude toward life and its possibilities

_____ in my level of ability to grow and change

Other change _____

_____ Heart Massage

Nurturing Wellness Journal Page

Day # _____ **Desired Outcome** _____

My Mood today is (check all that apply):

Good _____ Flat (Blah) _____ Depressed _____ Very depressed _____

Content _____ Erratic _____ Slightly Manic _____ Highly Manic _____

Angry _____ Anxious/fearful _____ Joyful _____ Hopeful _____

I woke up feeling rested today _____

Gratitude for today _____

I noticed the following emotions, body sensations, and thoughts *before* **the session** (list below):

Affirmation Group (if choosing a group): _____

After the session I noticed (place an X beside each YES answer):

_____ I was relaxed _____ I felt positive about my experience

_____ I was agitated / anxious _____ One or more of the affirmations challenged me

(Optional) Each day you have the option to choose one affirmation from your list for in-depth work.
Affirmation _____

SUDS: Subjective Units of Distress
Rate your distress on a scale between 0 (low) and 10 (high). Aim to achieve an ending SUDS of 2 or below.

Beginning **SUDS** level _____ Ending **SUDS** level _____

I notice that my daily sessions are creating positive changes (place an X beside each YES answer):

_____ in my relationship with others _____ in my relationship with myself

_____ in my self-care program _____ in my perception of my health / wellness

_____ in my ability to work through challenging issues and emotions

_____ in my confidence level and my feelings of self-worth

_____ in my daily activity level _____ in my perception of personal safety

_____ in my level of inner awareness _____ in my attitude toward life and its possibilities

_____ in my level of ability to grow and change

Other change _____

_____ Heart Massage

Nurturing Wellness Journal Page

Day # _____ **Desired Outcome** _____

My Mood today is (check all that apply):

Good _____	Flat (Blah) _____	Depressed _____	Very depressed _____
Content _____	Erratic _____	Slightly Manic _____	Highly Manic _____
Angry _____	Anxious/fearful _____	Joyful _____	Hopeful _____

I woke up feeling rested today _____

Gratitude for today _____

I noticed the following emotions, body sensations, and thoughts *before* the session (list below):

Affirmation Group (if choosing a group): _____

After the session I noticed (place an X beside each YES answer):

_____ I was relaxed   _____ I felt positive about my experience

_____ I was agitated / anxious   _____ One or more of the affirmations challenged me

(Optional) Each day you have the option to choose one affirmation from your list for in-depth work.
Affirmation _____

SUDS: Subjective Units of Distress
Rate your distress on a scale between 0 (low) and 10 (high). Aim to achieve an ending SUDS of 2 or below.

Beginning **SUDS** level _____   Ending **SUDS** level _____

I notice that my daily sessions are creating positive changes (place an X beside each YES answer):

_____ in my relationship with others   _____ in my relationship with myself

_____ in my self-care program   _____ in my perception of my health / wellness

_____ in my ability to work through challenging issues and emotions

_____ in my confidence level and my feelings of self-worth

_____ in my daily activity level   _____ in my perception of personal safety

_____ in my level of inner awareness   _____ in my attitude toward life and its possibilities

_____ in my level of ability to grow and change

Other change _____

_____ Heart Massage

Week 3: Trust the Process of life

Trusting yourself is trusting the wisdom that created you.
~ Wayne Dyer

Program: Daily Meditations or work with an Affirmation List
If using Affirmations, create your list below:

This Week's Insights

To be beautiful means to be yourself. You don't need to be accepted by others. You need to accept yourself.
~ Thich Nhat Hanh

Self-Care First!

Positive emotional and physical self-care is the most beautiful gift that you can give to yourself and your family. Put a check beside the activity on the days you engage in it. Meditation, at least once each week, is part of the Nurturing Wellness Through Radical Self-Care Program. The other listed activities are optional. Yoga and Tai Chi are good for energy flow. Yoga is great for depression and Tai Chi is great support for trauma survivors. Consider making one or both of them part of your rejuvenation program.

Meditation: _____ _____ _____ _____ _____ _____ _____

Meditation Journal: _____ _____ _____ _____ _____ _____ _____

Walking Meditation: _____ _____ _____ _____ _____ _____ _____

Breathing Meditation: _____ _____ _____ _____ _____ _____ _____

Exercise Walk: _____ _____ _____ _____ _____ _____ _____

Yoga: _____ _____ _____ _____ _____ _____ _____

Tai Chi: _____ _____ _____ _____ _____ _____ _____

Bubble Bath / Hot Tub: _____ _____ _____ _____ _____ _____ _____

Gym Workout: _____ _____ _____ _____ _____ _____ _____

Running or Jogging: _____ _____ _____ _____ _____ _____ _____

Team or Partner Sports: _____ _____ _____ _____ _____ _____ _____

Swimming: _____ _____ _____ _____ _____ _____ _____

Aerobics Class: _____ _____ _____ _____ _____ _____ _____

Massage and Body Work / Energy Healing: _____ _____ _____ _____ _____ _____ _____

Manicure or Pedicure: _____

Other: (List the activity or exercise below):

_____ : _____ _____ _____ _____ _____ _____ _____

_____ : _____ _____ _____ _____ _____ _____ _____

_____ : _____ _____ _____ _____ _____ _____ _____

Nurturing Wellness Journal Page

Day # _____ **Desired Outcome** _____

My Mood today is (check all that apply):

Good _____	Flat (Blah) _____	Depressed _____	Very depressed _____
Content _____	Erratic _____	Slightly Manic _____	Highly Manic _____
Angry _____	Anxious/fearful _____	Joyful _____	Hopeful _____

I woke up feeling rested today _____

Gratitude for today _____

I noticed the following emotions, body sensations, and thoughts *before* the session (list below):

Affirmation Group (if choosing a group): _____

After the session I noticed (place an X beside each YES answer):

_____ I was relaxed   _____ I felt positive about my experience

_____ I was agitated / anxious   _____ One or more of the affirmations challenged me

(Optional) Each day you have the option to choose one affirmation from your list for in-depth work.
Affirmation _____

SUDS: Subjective Units of Distress
Rate your distress on a scale between 0 (low) and 10 (high). Aim to achieve an ending SUDS of 2 or below.

Beginning **SUDS** level _____   Ending **SUDS** level _____

I notice that my daily sessions are creating positive changes (place an X beside each YES answer):

_____ in my relationship with others   _____ in my relationship with myself

_____ in my self-care program   _____ in my perception of my health / wellness

_____ in my ability to work through challenging issues and emotions

_____ in my confidence level and my feelings of self-worth

_____ in my daily activity level   _____ in my perception of personal safety

_____ in my level of inner awareness   _____ in my attitude toward life and its possibilities

_____ in my level of ability to grow and change

Other change _____

_____ Heart Massage

Nurturing Wellness Journal Page

Day # _____ **Desired Outcome** _____

My Mood today is (check all that apply):

Good	_____	Flat (Blah)	_____	Depressed	_____	Very depressed	_____
Content	_____	Erratic	_____	Slightly Manic	_____	Highly Manic	_____
Angry	_____	Anxious/fearful	_____	Joyful	_____	Hopeful	_____

I woke up feeling rested today _____

Gratitude for today _____

I noticed the following emotions, body sensations, and thoughts *before* the session (list below):

Affirmation Group (if choosing a group): _____

After the session I noticed (place an X beside each YES answer):

_____ I was relaxed   _____ I felt positive about my experience

_____ I was agitated / anxious   _____ One or more of the affirmations challenged me

> (Optional) Each day you have the option to choose one affirmation from your list for in-depth work.
> Affirmation _____
>
> **SUDS**: Subjective Units of Distress
> Rate your distress on a scale between 0 (low) and 10 (high). Aim to achieve an ending SUDS of 2 or below.
>
> Beginning **SUDS** level _____   Ending **SUDS** level _____

I notice that my daily sessions are creating positive changes (place an X beside each YES answer):

_____ in my relationship with others   _____ in my relationship with myself

_____ in my self-care program   _____ in my perception of my health / wellness

_____ in my ability to work through challenging issues and emotions

_____ in my confidence level and my feelings of self-worth

_____ in my daily activity level   _____ in my perception of personal safety

_____ in my level of inner awareness   _____ in my attitude toward life and its possibilities

_____ in my level of ability to grow and change

Other change _____

_____ Heart Massage

Nurturing Wellness Journal Page

Day # _____ **Desired Outcome** _____

My Mood today is (check all that apply):

Good _____	Flat (Blah) _____	Depressed _____	Very depressed _____
Content _____	Erratic _____	Slightly Manic _____	Highly Manic _____
Angry _____	Anxious/fearful _____	Joyful _____	Hopeful _____

I woke up feeling rested today _____

Gratitude for today _____

I noticed the following emotions, body sensations, and thoughts *before* the session (list below):

Affirmation Group (if choosing a group): _____

After the session I noticed (place an X beside each YES answer):

_____ I was relaxed _____ I felt positive about my experience

_____ I was agitated / anxious _____ One or more of the affirmations challenged me

(Optional) Each day you have the option to choose one affirmation from your list for in-depth work.
Affirmation _____

SUDS: Subjective Units of Distress
Rate your distress on a scale between 0 (low) and 10 (high). Aim to achieve an ending SUDS of 2 or below.

Beginning **SUDS** level _____ Ending **SUDS** level _____

I notice that my daily sessions are creating positive changes (place an X beside each YES answer):

_____ in my relationship with others _____ in my relationship with myself

_____ in my self-care program _____ in my perception of my health / wellness

_____ in my ability to work through challenging issues and emotions

_____ in my confidence level and my feelings of self-worth

_____ in my daily activity level _____ in my perception of personal safety

_____ in my level of inner awareness _____ in my attitude toward life and its possibilities

_____ in my level of ability to grow and change

Other change _____

_____ Heart Massage

Nurturing Wellness Journal Page

Day # _____   Desired Outcome _____

My Mood today is (check all that apply):

Good	_____	Flat (Blah)	_____	Depressed	_____	Very depressed	_____
Content	_____	Erratic	_____	Slightly Manic	_____	Highly Manic	_____
Angry	_____	Anxious/fearful	_____	Joyful	_____	Hopeful	_____

I woke up feeling rested today   _____

Gratitude for today _____

I noticed the following emotions, body sensations, and thoughts *before* **the session** (list below):

Affirmation Group (if choosing a group): _____

After the session I noticed (place an X beside each YES answer):

_____ I was relaxed   _____ I felt positive about my experience

_____ I was agitated / anxious   _____ One or more of the affirmations challenged me

(Optional) Each day you have the option to choose one affirmation from your list for in-depth work.
Affirmation _____

SUDS: Subjective Units of Distress
Rate your distress on a scale between 0 (low) and 10 (high). Aim to achieve an ending SUDS of 2 or below.

Beginning **SUDS** level _____   Ending **SUDS** level _____

I notice that my daily sessions are creating positive changes (place an X beside each YES answer):

_____ in my relationship with others   _____ in my relationship with myself

_____ in my self-care program   _____ in my perception of my health / wellness

_____ in my ability to work through challenging issues and emotions

_____ in my confidence level and my feelings of self-worth

_____ in my daily activity level   _____ in my perception of personal safety

_____ in my level of inner awareness   _____ in my attitude toward life and its possibilities

_____ in my level of ability to grow and change

Other change _____

_____ Heart Massage

Nurturing Wellness Journal Page

Day # _____ **Desired Outcome** _____

My Mood today is (check all that apply):

Good _____	Flat (Blah) _____	Depressed _____	Very depressed _____
Content _____	Erratic _____	Slightly Manic _____	Highly Manic _____
Angry _____	Anxious/fearful _____	Joyful _____	Hopeful _____

I woke up feeling rested today   _____

Gratitude for today _____

I noticed the following emotions, body sensations, and thoughts _before_ the session (list below):

Affirmation Group (if choosing a group): _____

After the session I noticed (place an X beside each YES answer):

_____ I was relaxed   _____ I felt positive about my experience

_____ I was agitated / anxious   _____ One or more of the affirmations challenged me

(Optional) Each day you have the option to choose one affirmation from your list for in-depth work.
Affirmation _____

SUDS: Subjective Units of Distress
Rate your distress on a scale between 0 (low) and 10 (high). Aim to achieve an ending SUDS of 2 or below.

Beginning **SUDS** level _____   Ending **SUDS** level _____

I notice that my daily sessions are creating positive changes (place an X beside each YES answer):

_____ in my relationship with others   _____ in my relationship with myself

_____ in my self-care program   _____ in my perception of my health / wellness

_____ in my ability to work through challenging issues and emotions

_____ in my confidence level and my feelings of self-worth

_____ in my daily activity level   _____ in my perception of personal safety

_____ in my level of inner awareness   _____ in my attitude toward life and its possibilities

_____ in my level of ability to grow and change

Other change _____

_____ Heart Massage

Week 4: Live a Now-Focused Life

The sun's energy warms the world, but when you focus it through a magnifying glass it can start a fire. Focus is so powerful!
~ Alan Parisir

Program: Daily Meditations or work with an Affirmation List
If using Affirmations, create your list below:

This Week's Insights

Most of the shadows in this life are caused by standing in one's own sunshine.
~ Ralph Waldo Emerson

Self-Care First!

Positive emotional and physical self-care is the most beautiful gift that you can give to yourself and your family. Put a check beside the activity on the days you engage in it. Meditation, at least once each week, is part of the Nurturing Wellness Through Radical Self-Care Program. The other listed activities are optional. Yoga and Tai Chi are good for energy flow. Yoga is great for depression and Tai Chi is great support for trauma survivors. Consider making one or both of them part of your rejuvenation program.

Meditation: ____ ____ ____ ____ ____ ____ ____

Meditation Journal: ____ ____ ____ ____ ____ ____ ____

Walking Meditation: ____ ____ ____ ____ ____ ____ ____

Breathing Meditation: ____ ____ ____ ____ ____ ____ ____

Exercise Walk: ____ ____ ____ ____ ____ ____ ____

Yoga: ____ ____ ____ ____ ____ ____ ____

Tai Chi: ____ ____ ____ ____ ____ ____ ____

Bubble Bath / Hot Tub: ____ ____ ____ ____ ____ ____ ____

Gym Workout: ____ ____ ____ ____ ____ ____ ____

Running or Jogging: ____ ____ ____ ____ ____ ____ ____

Team or Partner Sports: ____ ____ ____ ____ ____ ____ ____

Swimming: ____ ____ ____ ____ ____ ____ ____

Aerobics Class: ____ ____ ____ ____ ____ ____ ____

Massage and Body Work / Energy Healing: ____ ____ ____ ____ ____ ____ ____

Manicure or Pedicure: ____

Other: (List the activity or exercise below):

_____ : ____ ____ ____ ____ ____ ____ ____

_____ : ____ ____ ____ ____ ____ ____ ____

_____ : ____ ____ ____ ____ ____ ____ ____

Nurturing Wellness Journal Page

Day # _____   **Desired Outcome** _____

My Mood today is (check all that apply):

Good _____	Flat (Blah) _____	Depressed _____	Very depressed _____
Content _____	Erratic _____	Slightly Manic _____	Highly Manic _____
Angry _____	Anxious/fearful _____	Joyful _____	Hopeful _____

I woke up feeling rested today   _____

Gratitude for today _____

I noticed the following emotions, body sensations, and thoughts *before* **the session** (list below):

Affirmation Group (if choosing a group): _____

After the session I noticed (place an X beside each YES answer):

_____ I was relaxed   _____ I felt positive about my experience

_____ I was agitated / anxious   _____ One or more of the affirmations challenged me

(Optional) Each day you have the option to choose one affirmation from your list for in-depth work.
Affirmation _____

SUDS: Subjective Units of Distress
Rate your distress on a scale between 0 (low) and 10 (high). Aim to achieve an ending SUDS of 2 or below.

Beginning **SUDS** level _____   Ending **SUDS** level _____

I notice that my daily sessions are creating positive changes (place an X beside each YES answer):

_____ in my relationship with others   _____ in my relationship with myself
_____ in my self-care program   _____ in my perception of my health / wellness
_____ in my ability to work through challenging issues and emotions
_____ in my confidence level and my feelings of self-worth
_____ in my daily activity level   _____ in my perception of personal safety
_____ in my level of inner awareness   _____ in my attitude toward life and its possibilities
_____ in my level of ability to grow and change

Other change _____

_____ Heart Massage

Nurturing Wellness Journal Page

Day # _____ **Desired Outcome** _____

My Mood today is (check all that apply):

Good	_____	Flat (Blah)	_____	Depressed	_____	Very depressed	_____
Content	_____	Erratic	_____	Slightly Manic	_____	Highly Manic	_____
Angry	_____	Anxious/fearful	_____	Joyful	_____	Hopeful	_____

I woke up feeling rested today _____

Gratitude for today _____

I noticed the following emotions, body sensations, and thoughts *before* **the session** (list below):

Affirmation Group (if choosing a group): _____

After the session I noticed (place an X beside each YES answer):

_____ I was relaxed   _____ I felt positive about my experience

_____ I was agitated / anxious   _____ One or more of the affirmations challenged me

(Optional) Each day you have the option to choose one affirmation from your list for in-depth work.
Affirmation _____

SUDS: Subjective Units of Distress
Rate your distress on a scale between 0 (low) and 10 (high). Aim to achieve an ending SUDS of 2 or below.

Beginning **SUDS** level _____   Ending **SUDS** level _____

I notice that my daily sessions are creating positive changes (place an X beside each YES answer):

_____ in my relationship with others   _____ in my relationship with myself

_____ in my self-care program   _____ in my perception of my health / wellness

_____ in my ability to work through challenging issues and emotions

_____ in my confidence level and my feelings of self-worth

_____ in my daily activity level   _____ in my perception of personal safety

_____ in my level of inner awareness   _____ in my attitude toward life and its possibilities

_____ in my level of ability to grow and change

Other change _____

_____ Heart Massage

Nurturing Wellness Journal Page

Day # _____ **Desired Outcome** _____

My Mood today is (check all that apply):

Good _____ Flat (Blah) _____ Depressed _____ Very depressed _____

Content _____ Erratic _____ Slightly Manic _____ Highly Manic _____

Angry _____ Anxious/fearful _____ Joyful _____ Hopeful _____

I woke up feeling rested today _____

Gratitude for today _____

I noticed the following emotions, body sensations, and thoughts *before* **the session** (list below):

Affirmation Group (if choosing a group): _____

After the session I noticed (place an X beside each YES answer):

_____ I was relaxed   _____ I felt positive about my experience

_____ I was agitated / anxious   _____ One or more of the affirmations challenged me

(Optional) Each day you have the option to choose one affirmation from your list for in-depth work.
Affirmation _____

SUDS: Subjective Units of Distress
Rate your distress on a scale between 0 (low) and 10 (high). Aim to achieve an ending SUDS of 2 or below.

Beginning **SUDS** level _____   Ending **SUDS** level _____

I notice that my daily sessions are creating positive changes (place an X beside each YES answer):

_____ in my relationship with others   _____ in my relationship with myself

_____ in my self-care program   _____ in my perception of my health / wellness

_____ in my ability to work through challenging issues and emotions

_____ in my confidence level and my feelings of self-worth

_____ in my daily activity level   _____ in my perception of personal safety

_____ in my level of inner awareness   _____ in my attitude toward life and its possibilities

_____ in my level of ability to grow and change

Other change _____

_____ Heart Massage

Nurturing Wellness Journal Page

Day # _____ **Desired Outcome** _____

My Mood today is (check all that apply):

Good	_____	Flat (Blah)	_____	Depressed	_____	Very depressed	_____
Content	_____	Erratic	_____	Slightly Manic	_____	Highly Manic	_____
Angry	_____	Anxious/fearful	_____	Joyful	_____	Hopeful	_____

I woke up feeling rested today   _____

Gratitude for today _____

I noticed the following emotions, body sensations, and thoughts *before* the session (list below):

Affirmation Group (if choosing a group): _____

After the session I noticed (place an X beside each YES answer):

_____ I was relaxed   _____ I felt positive about my experience

_____ I was agitated / anxious   _____ One or more of the affirmations challenged me

(Optional) Each day you have the option to choose one affirmation from your list for in-depth work.
Affirmation _____

SUDS: Subjective Units of Distress
Rate your distress on a scale between 0 (low) and 10 (high). Aim to achieve an ending SUDS of 2 or below.

Beginning **SUDS** level _____   Ending **SUDS** level _____

I notice that my daily sessions are creating positive changes (place an X beside each YES answer):

_____ in my relationship with others   _____ in my relationship with myself

_____ in my self-care program   _____ in my perception of my health / wellness

_____ in my ability to work through challenging issues and emotions

_____ in my confidence level and my feelings of self-worth

_____ in my daily activity level   _____ in my perception of personal safety

_____ in my level of inner awareness   _____ in my attitude toward life and its possibilities

_____ in my level of ability to grow and change

Other change _____

_____ Heart Massage

Nurturing Wellness Journal Page

Day # _____ **Desired Outcome** _____

My Mood today is (check all that apply):

Good _____	Flat (Blah) _____	Depressed _____	Very depressed _____
Content _____	Erratic _____	Slightly Manic _____	Highly Manic _____
Angry _____	Anxious/fearful _____	Joyful _____	Hopeful _____

I woke up feeling rested today _____

Gratitude for today _____

I noticed the following emotions, body sensations, and thoughts *before* **the session** (list below):

Affirmation Group (if choosing a group): _____

After the session I noticed (place an X beside each YES answer):

_____ I was relaxed _____ I felt positive about my experience

_____ I was agitated / anxious _____ One or more of the affirmations challenged me

(Optional) Each day you have the option to choose one affirmation from your list for in-depth work.
Affirmation _____

SUDS: Subjective Units of Distress
Rate your distress on a scale between 0 (low) and 10 (high). Aim to achieve an ending SUDS of 2 or below.

Beginning **SUDS** level _____ Ending **SUDS** level _____

I notice that my daily sessions are creating positive changes (place an X beside each YES answer):

_____ in my relationship with others _____ in my relationship with myself

_____ in my self-care program _____ in my perception of my health / wellness

_____ in my ability to work through challenging issues and emotions

_____ in my confidence level and my feelings of self-worth

_____ in my daily activity level _____ in my perception of personal safety

_____ in my level of inner awareness _____ in my attitude toward life and its possibilities

_____ in my level of ability to grow and change

Other change _____

_____ Heart Massage

Week 5: Laugh Often

At the height of laughter, the universe is flung into a kaleidoscope of new possibilities.
~ Jean Houston

Program: Daily Meditations or work with an Affirmation List
If using Affirmations, create your list below:

This Week's Insights

The privilege of a lifetime is being who you are.
~ Joseph Campbell

Self-Care First!

Positive emotional and physical self-care is the most beautiful gift that you can give to yourself and your family. Put a check beside the activity on the days you engage in it. Meditation, at least once each week, is part of the Nurturing Wellness Through Radical Self-Care Program. The other listed activities are optional. Yoga and Tai Chi are good for energy flow. Yoga is great for depression and Tai Chi is great support for trauma survivors. Consider making one or both of them part of your rejuvenation program.

Meditation: ____ ____ ____ ____ ____ ____ ____

Meditation Journal: ____ ____ ____ ____ ____ ____ ____

Walking Meditation: ____ ____ ____ ____ ____ ____ ____

Breathing Meditation: ____ ____ ____ ____ ____ ____ ____

Exercise Walk: ____ ____ ____ ____ ____ ____ ____

Yoga: ____ ____ ____ ____ ____ ____ ____

Tai Chi: ____ ____ ____ ____ ____ ____ ____

Bubble Bath / Hot Tub: ____ ____ ____ ____ ____ ____ ____

Gym Workout: ____ ____ ____ ____ ____ ____ ____

Running or Jogging: ____ ____ ____ ____ ____ ____ ____

Team or Partner Sports: ____ ____ ____ ____ ____ ____ ____

Swimming: ____ ____ ____ ____ ____ ____ ____

Aerobics Class: ____ ____ ____ ____ ____ ____ ____

Massage and Body Work / Energy Healing: ____ ____ ____ ____ ____ ____ ____

Manicure or Pedicure: ____

Other: (List the activity or exercise below):

_____ : ____ ____ ____ ____ ____ ____ ____

_____ : ____ ____ ____ ____ ____ ____ ____

_____ : ____ ____ ____ ____ ____ ____ ____

Nurturing Wellness Journal Page

Day # _____   **Desired Outcome** _____

My Mood today is (check all that apply):

Good _____	Flat (Blah) _____	Depressed _____	Very depressed _____
Content _____	Erratic _____	Slightly Manic _____	Highly Manic _____
Angry _____	Anxious/fearful _____	Joyful _____	Hopeful _____

I woke up feeling rested today _____

Gratitude for today _____

I noticed the following emotions, body sensations, and thoughts *before* **the session** (list below):

Affirmation Group (if choosing a group): _____

After the session I noticed (place an X beside each YES answer):

_____ I was relaxed _____ I felt positive about my experience

_____ I was agitated / anxious _____ One or more of the affirmations challenged me

(Optional) Each day you have the option to choose one affirmation from your list for in-depth work.
Affirmation _____

SUDS: Subjective Units of Distress
Rate your distress on a scale between 0 (low) and 10 (high). Aim to achieve an ending SUDS of 2 or below.

Beginning **SUDS** level _____ Ending **SUDS** level _____

I notice that my daily sessions are creating positive changes (place an X beside each YES answer):

_____ in my relationship with others _____ in my relationship with myself

_____ in my self-care program _____ in my perception of my health / wellness

_____ in my ability to work through challenging issues and emotions

_____ in my confidence level and my feelings of self-worth

_____ in my daily activity level _____ in my perception of personal safety

_____ in my level of inner awareness _____ in my attitude toward life and its possibilities

_____ in my level of ability to grow and change

Other change _____

_____ Heart Massage

Nurturing Wellness Journal Page

Day # _____   **Desired Outcome** _____

My Mood today is (check all that apply):

Good _____	Flat (Blah) _____	Depressed _____	Very depressed _____
Content _____	Erratic _____	Slightly Manic _____	Highly Manic _____
Angry _____	Anxious/fearful _____	Joyful _____	Hopeful _____

I woke up feeling rested today   _____

Gratitude for today _____

I noticed the following emotions, body sensations, and thoughts *before* **the session** (list below):

Affirmation Group (if choosing a group): _____

After the session I noticed (place an X beside each YES answer):

_____ I was relaxed   _____ I felt positive about my experience

_____ I was agitated / anxious   _____ One or more of the affirmations challenged me

(Optional) Each day you have the option to choose one affirmation from your list for in-depth work.
Affirmation _____

SUDS: Subjective Units of Distress
Rate your distress on a scale between 0 (low) and 10 (high). Aim to achieve an ending SUDS of 2 or below.

Beginning **SUDS** level _____   Ending **SUDS** level _____

I notice that my daily sessions are creating positive changes (place an X beside each YES answer):

_____ in my relationship with others   _____ in my relationship with myself

_____ in my self-care program   _____ in my perception of my health / wellness

_____ in my ability to work through challenging issues and emotions

_____ in my confidence level and my feelings of self-worth

_____ in my daily activity level   _____ in my perception of personal safety

_____ in my level of inner awareness   _____ in my attitude toward life and its possibilities

_____ in my level of ability to grow and change

Other change _____

_____ Heart Massage

Nurturing Wellness Journal Page

Day # _____   **Desired Outcome** _____

My Mood today is (check all that apply):

Good _____	Flat (Blah) _____	Depressed _____	Very depressed _____
Content _____	Erratic _____	Slightly Manic _____	Highly Manic _____
Angry _____	Anxious/fearful _____	Joyful _____	Hopeful _____

I woke up feeling rested today   _____

Gratitude for today _____

I noticed the following emotions, body sensations, and thoughts *before* the session (list below):

Affirmation Group (if choosing a group): _____

After the session I noticed (place an X beside each YES answer):

_____ I was relaxed   _____ I felt positive about my experience

_____ I was agitated / anxious   _____ One or more of the affirmations challenged me

(Optional) Each day you have the option to choose one affirmation from your list for in-depth work.
Affirmation _____

SUDS: Subjective Units of Distress
Rate your distress on a scale between 0 (low) and 10 (high). Aim to achieve an ending SUDS of 2 or below.

Beginning **SUDS** level _____   Ending **SUDS** level _____

I notice that my daily sessions are creating positive changes (place an X beside each YES answer):

_____ in my relationship with others   _____ in my relationship with myself
_____ in my self-care program   _____ in my perception of my health / wellness
_____ in my ability to work through challenging issues and emotions
_____ in my confidence level and my feelings of self-worth
_____ in my daily activity level   _____ in my perception of personal safety
_____ in my level of inner awareness   _____ in my attitude toward life and its possibilities
_____ in my level of ability to grow and change

Other change _____

_____ Heart Massage

Nurturing Wellness Journal Page

Day # _____   **Desired Outcome** _____

My Mood today is (check all that apply):

Good _____	Flat (Blah) _____	Depressed _____	Very depressed _____
Content _____	Erratic _____	Slightly Manic _____	Highly Manic _____
Angry _____	Anxious/fearful _____	Joyful _____	Hopeful _____

I woke up feeling rested today   _____

Gratitude for today _____

I noticed the following emotions, body sensations, and thoughts *before* the session (list below):

Affirmation Group (if choosing a group): _____

After the session I noticed (place an X beside each YES answer):

_____ I was relaxed   _____ I felt positive about my experience

_____ I was agitated / anxious   _____ One or more of the affirmations challenged me

(Optional) Each day you have the option to choose one affirmation from your list for in-depth work.
Affirmation _____

SUDS: Subjective Units of Distress
Rate your distress on a scale between 0 (low) and 10 (high). Aim to achieve an ending SUDS of 2 or below.

Beginning **SUDS** level _____   Ending **SUDS** level _____

I notice that my daily sessions are creating positive changes (place an X beside each YES answer):

_____ in my relationship with others   _____ in my relationship with myself

_____ in my self-care program   _____ in my perception of my health / wellness

_____ in my ability to work through challenging issues and emotions

_____ in my confidence level and my feelings of self-worth

_____ in my daily activity level   _____ in my perception of personal safety

_____ in my level of inner awareness   _____ in my attitude toward life and its possibilities

_____ in my level of ability to grow and change

Other change _____

_____ Heart Massage

Nurturing Wellness Journal Page

Day # _____   **Desired Outcome** _____

My Mood today is (check all that apply):

Good _____	Flat (Blah) _____	Depressed _____	Very depressed _____
Content _____	Erratic _____	Slightly Manic _____	Highly Manic _____
Angry _____	Anxious/fearful _____	Joyful _____	Hopeful _____

I woke up feeling rested today   _____

Gratitude for today _____

I noticed the following emotions, body sensations, and thoughts *before* **the session** (list below):

Affirmation Group (if choosing a group): _____

After the session I noticed (place an X beside each YES answer):

_____ I was relaxed   _____ I felt positive about my experience

_____ I was agitated / anxious   _____ One or more of the affirmations challenged me

(Optional) Each day you have the option to choose one affirmation from your list for in-depth work.
Affirmation _____

SUDS: Subjective Units of Distress
Rate your distress on a scale between 0 (low) and 10 (high). Aim to achieve an ending SUDS of 2 or below.

Beginning **SUDS** level _____   Ending **SUDS** level _____

I notice that my daily sessions are creating positive changes (place an X beside each YES answer):

_____ in my relationship with others   _____ in my relationship with myself
_____ in my self-care program   _____ in my perception of my health / wellness
_____ in my ability to work through challenging issues and emotions
_____ in my confidence level and my feelings of self-worth
_____ in my daily activity level   _____ in my perception of personal safety
_____ in my level of inner awareness   _____ in my attitude toward life and its possibilities
_____ in my level of ability to grow and change

Other change _____

_____ Heart Massage

Week 6: Trust, Love, and Forgive

May the stars carry your sadness away,
May the flowers fill your heart with beauty,
May hope forever wipe away your tears,
And, above all, may silence make you strong.
~ Chief Dan George

Program: Daily Meditations or work with an Affirmation List
If using Affirmations, create your list below:

This Week's Insights

Put all excuses aside and remember this: You are capable.
~ Zig Ziglar

Self-Care First!

Positive emotional and physical self-care is the most beautiful gift that you can give to yourself and your family. Put a check beside the activity on the days you engage in it. Meditation, at least once each week, is part of the Nurturing Wellness Through Radical Self-Care Program. The other listed activities are optional. Yoga and Tai Chi are good for energy flow. Yoga is great for depression and Tai Chi is great support for trauma survivors. Consider making one or both of them part of your rejuvenation program.

Meditation: ____ ____ ____ ____ ____ ____ ____

Meditation Journal: ____ ____ ____ ____ ____ ____ ____

Walking Meditation: ____ ____ ____ ____ ____ ____ ____

Breathing Meditation: ____ ____ ____ ____ ____ ____ ____

Exercise Walk: ____ ____ ____ ____ ____ ____ ____

Yoga: ____ ____ ____ ____ ____ ____ ____

Tai Chi: ____ ____ ____ ____ ____ ____ ____

Bubble Bath / Hot Tub: ____ ____ ____ ____ ____ ____ ____

Gym Workout: ____ ____ ____ ____ ____ ____ ____

Running or Jogging: ____ ____ ____ ____ ____ ____ ____

Team or Partner Sports: ____ ____ ____ ____ ____ ____ ____

Swimming: ____ ____ ____ ____ ____ ____ ____

Aerobics Class: ____ ____ ____ ____ ____ ____ ____

Massage and Body Work / Energy Healing: ____ ____ ____ ____ ____ ____ ____

Manicure or Pedicure: ____

Other: (List the activity or exercise below):

_____ : ____ ____ ____ ____ ____ ____ ____

_____ : ____ ____ ____ ____ ____ ____ ____

_____ : ____ ____ ____ ____ ____ ____ ____

Nurturing Wellness Journal Page

Day # _____ **Desired Outcome** _____

My Mood today is (check all that apply):

Good _____	Flat (Blah) _____	Depressed _____	Very depressed _____
Content _____	Erratic _____	Slightly Manic _____	Highly Manic _____
Angry _____	Anxious/fearful _____	Joyful _____	Hopeful _____

I woke up feeling rested today _____

Gratitude for today _____

I noticed the following emotions, body sensations, and thoughts *before* **the session** (list below):

Affirmation Group (if choosing a group): _____

After the session I noticed (place an X beside each YES answer):

_____ I was relaxed   _____ I felt positive about my experience

_____ I was agitated / anxious   _____ One or more of the affirmations challenged me

(Optional) Each day you have the option to choose one affirmation from your list for in-depth work.
Affirmation _____

SUDS: Subjective Units of Distress
Rate your distress on a scale between 0 (low) and 10 (high). Aim to achieve an ending SUDS of 2 or below.

Beginning **SUDS** level _____   Ending **SUDS** level _____

I notice that my daily sessions are creating positive changes (place an X beside each YES answer):

_____ in my relationship with others   _____ in my relationship with myself
_____ in my self-care program   _____ in my perception of my health / wellness
_____ in my ability to work through challenging issues and emotions
_____ in my confidence level and my feelings of self-worth
_____ in my daily activity level   _____ in my perception of personal safety
_____ in my level of inner awareness   _____ in my attitude toward life and its possibilities
_____ in my level of ability to grow and change

Other change _____

_____ Heart Massage

Nurturing Wellness Journal Page

Day # _____ **Desired Outcome** _____

My Mood today is (check all that apply):

Good _____	Flat (Blah) _____	Depressed _____	Very depressed _____
Content _____	Erratic _____	Slightly Manic _____	Highly Manic _____
Angry _____	Anxious/fearful _____	Joyful _____	Hopeful _____

I woke up feeling rested today   _____

Gratitude for today _____

I noticed the following emotions, body sensations, and thoughts *before* the session (list below):

Affirmation Group (if choosing a group): _____

After the session I noticed (place an X beside each YES answer):

_____ I was relaxed   _____ I felt positive about my experience

_____ I was agitated / anxious   _____ One or more of the affirmations challenged me

(Optional) Each day you have the option to choose one affirmation from your list for in-depth work.
Affirmation _____

SUDS: Subjective Units of Distress
Rate your distress on a scale between 0 (low) and 10 (high). Aim to achieve an ending SUDS of 2 or below.

Beginning **SUDS** level _____   Ending **SUDS** level _____

I notice that my daily sessions are creating positive changes (place an X beside each YES answer):

_____ in my relationship with others   _____ in my relationship with myself

_____ in my self-care program   _____ in my perception of my health / wellness

_____ in my ability to work through challenging issues and emotions

_____ in my confidence level and my feelings of self-worth

_____ in my daily activity level   _____ in my perception of personal safety

_____ in my level of inner awareness   _____ in my attitude toward life and its possibilities

_____ in my level of ability to grow and change

Other change _____

_____ Heart Massage

Nurturing Wellness Journal Page

Day # _____   **Desired Outcome** _____

My Mood today is (check all that apply):

Good _____	Flat (Blah) _____	Depressed _____	Very depressed _____
Content _____	Erratic _____	Slightly Manic _____	Highly Manic _____
Angry _____	Anxious/fearful _____	Joyful _____	Hopeful _____

I woke up feeling rested today   _____

Gratitude for today _____

I noticed the following emotions, body sensations, and thoughts *before* **the session** (list below):

Affirmation Group (if choosing a group): _____

After the session I noticed (place an X beside each YES answer):

_____ I was relaxed   _____ I felt positive about my experience

_____ I was agitated / anxious   _____ One or more of the affirmations challenged me

(Optional) Each day you have the option to choose one affirmation from your list for in-depth work.
Affirmation _____

SUDS: Subjective Units of Distress
Rate your distress on a scale between 0 (low) and 10 (high). Aim to achieve an ending SUDS of 2 or below.

Beginning **SUDS** level _____   Ending **SUDS** level _____

I notice that my daily sessions are creating positive changes (place an X beside each YES answer):

_____ in my relationship with others   _____ in my relationship with myself

_____ in my self-care program   _____ in my perception of my health / wellness

_____ in my ability to work through challenging issues and emotions

_____ in my confidence level and my feelings of self-worth

_____ in my daily activity level   _____ in my perception of personal safety

_____ in my level of inner awareness   _____ in my attitude toward life and its possibilities

_____ in my level of ability to grow and change

Other change _____

_____ Heart Massage

Nurturing Wellness Journal Page

Day # _____   **Desired Outcome** _____

My Mood today is (check all that apply):

Good _____   Flat (Blah) _____   Depressed _____   Very depressed _____

Content _____   Erratic _____   Slightly Manic _____   Highly Manic _____

Angry _____   Anxious/fearful _____   Joyful _____   Hopeful _____

I woke up feeling rested today _____

Gratitude for today _____

I noticed the following emotions, body sensations, and thoughts *before* **the session** (list below):

Affirmation Group (if choosing a group): _____

After the session I noticed (place an X beside each YES answer):

_____ I was relaxed   _____ I felt positive about my experience

_____ I was agitated / anxious   _____ One or more of the affirmations challenged me

(Optional) Each day you have the option to choose one affirmation from your list for in-depth work.
Affirmation _____

SUDS: Subjective Units of Distress
Rate your distress on a scale between 0 (low) and 10 (high). Aim to achieve an ending SUDS of 2 or below.

Beginning **SUDS** level _____   Ending **SUDS** level _____

I notice that my daily sessions are creating positive changes (place an X beside each YES answer):

_____ in my relationship with others   _____ in my relationship with myself

_____ in my self-care program   _____ in my perception of my health / wellness

_____ in my ability to work through challenging issues and emotions

_____ in my confidence level and my feelings of self-worth

_____ in my daily activity level   _____ in my perception of personal safety

_____ in my level of inner awareness   _____ in my attitude toward life and its possibilities

_____ in my level of ability to grow and change

Other change _____

_____ Heart Massage

Nurturing Wellness Journal Page

Day # _____ **Desired Outcome** _____

My Mood today is (check all that apply):

Good _____	Flat (Blah) _____	Depressed _____	Very depressed _____
Content _____	Erratic _____	Slightly Manic _____	Highly Manic _____
Angry _____	Anxious/fearful _____	Joyful _____	Hopeful _____

I woke up feeling rested today   _____

Gratitude for today _____

I noticed the following emotions, body sensations, and thoughts *before* **the session** (list below):

Affirmation Group (if choosing a group): _____

After the session I noticed (place an X beside each YES answer):

_____ I was relaxed   _____ I felt positive about my experience

_____ I was agitated / anxious   _____ One or more of the affirmations challenged me

(Optional) Each day you have the option to choose one affirmation from your list for in-depth work.
Affirmation _____

SUDS: Subjective Units of Distress
Rate your distress on a scale between 0 (low) and 10 (high). Aim to achieve an ending SUDS of 2 or below.

Beginning **SUDS** level _____   Ending **SUDS** level _____

I notice that my daily sessions are creating positive changes (place an X beside each YES answer):

_____ in my relationship with others   _____ in my relationship with myself

_____ in my self-care program   _____ in my perception of my health / wellness

_____ in my ability to work through challenging issues and emotions

_____ in my confidence level and my feelings of self-worth

_____ in my daily activity level   _____ in my perception of personal safety

_____ in my level of inner awareness   _____ in my attitude toward life and its possibilities

_____ in my level of ability to grow and change

Other change _____

_____ Heart Massage

Week 7: I Am Worthy

Don't you dare, for one more second, surround yourself with people who are not aware of the greatness that you are.
~ Jo Blackwell-Preston

Program: Daily Meditations or work with an Affirmation List
If using Affirmations, create your list below:

This Week's Insights

The most terrifying thing is to accept oneself completely.
~ Carl Jung

Self-Care First!

Positive emotional and physical self-care is the most beautiful gift that you can give to yourself and your family. Put a check beside the activity on the days you engage in it. Meditation, at least once each week, is part of the Nurturing Wellness Through Radical Self-Care Program. The other listed activities are optional. Yoga and Tai Chi are good for energy flow. Yoga is great for depression and Tai Chi is great support for trauma survivors. Consider making one or both of them part of your rejuvenation program.

Meditation: ____ ____ ____ ____ ____ ____ ____

Meditation Journal: ____ ____ ____ ____ ____ ____ ____

Walking Meditation: ____ ____ ____ ____ ____ ____ ____

Breathing Meditation: ____ ____ ____ ____ ____ ____ ____

Exercise Walk: ____ ____ ____ ____ ____ ____ ____

Yoga: ____ ____ ____ ____ ____ ____ ____

Tai Chi: ____ ____ ____ ____ ____ ____ ____

Bubble Bath / Hot Tub: ____ ____ ____ ____ ____ ____ ____

Gym Workout: ____ ____ ____ ____ ____ ____ ____

Running or Jogging: ____ ____ ____ ____ ____ ____ ____

Team or Partner Sports: ____ ____ ____ ____ ____ ____ ____

Swimming: ____ ____ ____ ____ ____ ____ ____

Aerobics Class: ____ ____ ____ ____ ____ ____ ____

Massage and Body Work / Energy Healing: ____ ____ ____ ____ ____ ____ ____

Manicure or Pedicure: ____

Other: (List the activity or exercise below):

_____ : ____ ____ ____ ____ ____ ____ ____

_____ : ____ ____ ____ ____ ____ ____ ____

_____ : ____ ____ ____ ____ ____ ____ ____

Nurturing Wellness Journal Page

Day # _____ **Desired Outcome** _____

My Mood today is (check all that apply):

Good _____	Flat (Blah) _____	Depressed _____	Very depressed _____
Content _____	Erratic _____	Slightly Manic _____	Highly Manic _____
Angry _____	Anxious/fearful _____	Joyful _____	Hopeful _____

I woke up feeling rested today _____

Gratitude for today _____

I noticed the following emotions, body sensations, and thoughts *before* the session (list below):

Affirmation Group (if choosing a group): _____

After the session I noticed (place an X beside each YES answer):

_____ I was relaxed _____ I felt positive about my experience

_____ I was agitated / anxious _____ One or more of the affirmations challenged me

(Optional) Each day you have the option to choose one affirmation from your list for in-depth work.
Affirmation _____

SUDS: Subjective Units of Distress
Rate your distress on a scale between 0 (low) and 10 (high). Aim to achieve an ending SUDS of 2 or below.

Beginning **SUDS** level _____ Ending **SUDS** level _____

I notice that my daily sessions are creating positive changes (place an X beside each YES answer):

_____ in my relationship with others _____ in my relationship with myself

_____ in my self-care program _____ in my perception of my health / wellness

_____ in my ability to work through challenging issues and emotions

_____ in my confidence level and my feelings of self-worth

_____ in my daily activity level _____ in my perception of personal safety

_____ in my level of inner awareness _____ in my attitude toward life and its possibilities

_____ in my level of ability to grow and change

Other change _____

_____ Heart Massage

Nurturing Wellness Journal Page

Day # _____ **Desired Outcome** _____

My Mood today is (check all that apply):

Good _____	Flat (Blah) _____	Depressed _____	Very depressed _____
Content _____	Erratic _____	Slightly Manic _____	Highly Manic _____
Angry _____	Anxious/fearful _____	Joyful _____	Hopeful _____

I woke up feeling rested today _____

Gratitude for today _____

I noticed the following emotions, body sensations, and thoughts *before* **the session** (list below):

Affirmation Group (if choosing a group): _____

After the session I noticed (place an X beside each YES answer):

_____ I was relaxed   _____ I felt positive about my experience

_____ I was agitated / anxious   _____ One or more of the affirmations challenged me

(Optional) Each day you have the option to choose one affirmation from your list for in-depth work.
Affirmation _____

SUDS: Subjective Units of Distress
Rate your distress on a scale between 0 (low) and 10 (high). Aim to achieve an ending SUDS of 2 or below.

Beginning **SUDS** level _____   Ending **SUDS** level _____

I notice that my daily sessions are creating positive changes (place an X beside each YES answer):

_____ in my relationship with others   _____ in my relationship with myself

_____ in my self-care program   _____ in my perception of my health / wellness

_____ in my ability to work through challenging issues and emotions

_____ in my confidence level and my feelings of self-worth

_____ in my daily activity level   _____ in my perception of personal safety

_____ in my level of inner awareness   _____ in my attitude toward life and its possibilities

_____ in my level of ability to grow and change

Other change _____

_____ Heart Massage

Nurturing Wellness Journal Page

Day # _____ **Desired Outcome** _____

My Mood today is (check all that apply):

Good _____	Flat (Blah) _____	Depressed _____	Very depressed _____
Content _____	Erratic _____	Slightly Manic _____	Highly Manic _____
Angry _____	Anxious/fearful _____	Joyful _____	Hopeful _____

I woke up feeling rested today _____

Gratitude for today _____

I noticed the following emotions, body sensations, and thoughts *before* the session (list below):

Affirmation Group (if choosing a group): _____

After the session I noticed (place an X beside each YES answer):

_____ I was relaxed   _____ I felt positive about my experience

_____ I was agitated / anxious   _____ One or more of the affirmations challenged me

(Optional) Each day you have the option to choose one affirmation from your list for in-depth work.
Affirmation _____

SUDS: Subjective Units of Distress
Rate your distress on a scale between 0 (low) and 10 (high). Aim to achieve an ending SUDS of 2 or below.

Beginning **SUDS** level _____   Ending **SUDS** level _____

I notice that my daily sessions are creating positive changes (place an X beside each YES answer):

_____ in my relationship with others   _____ in my relationship with myself

_____ in my self-care program   _____ in my perception of my health / wellness

_____ in my ability to work through challenging issues and emotions

_____ in my confidence level and my feelings of self-worth

_____ in my daily activity level   _____ in my perception of personal safety

_____ in my level of inner awareness   _____ in my attitude toward life and its possibilities

_____ in my level of ability to grow and change

Other change _____

_____ Heart Massage

Nurturing Wellness Journal Page

Day # _____   **Desired Outcome** _____

My Mood today is (check all that apply):

Good _____	Flat (Blah) _____	Depressed _____	Very depressed _____
Content _____	Erratic _____	Slightly Manic _____	Highly Manic _____
Angry _____	Anxious/fearful _____	Joyful _____	Hopeful _____

I woke up feeling rested today   _____

Gratitude for today _____

I noticed the following emotions, body sensations, and thoughts *before* **the session** (list below):

Affirmation Group (if choosing a group): _____

After the session I noticed (place an X beside each YES answer):

_____   I was relaxed   _____   I felt positive about my experience

_____   I was agitated / anxious   _____   One or more of the affirmations challenged me

(Optional) Each day you have the option to choose one affirmation from your list for in-depth work.
Affirmation _____

SUDS: Subjective Units of Distress
Rate your distress on a scale between 0 (low) and 10 (high). Aim to achieve an ending SUDS of 2 or below.

Beginning **SUDS** level _____   Ending **SUDS** level _____

I notice that my daily sessions are creating positive changes (place an X beside each YES answer):

_____   in my relationship with others   _____   in my relationship with myself

_____   in my self-care program   _____   in my perception of my health / wellness

_____   in my ability to work through challenging issues and emotions

_____   in my confidence level and my feelings of self-worth

_____   in my daily activity level   _____   in my perception of personal safety

_____   in my level of inner awareness   _____   in my attitude toward life and its possibilities

_____   in my level of ability to grow and change

Other change _____

_____   Heart Massage

Nurturing Wellness Journal Page

Day # _____ **Desired Outcome** _____

My Mood today is (check all that apply):

Good _____ Flat (Blah) _____ Depressed _____ Very depressed _____

Content _____ Erratic _____ Slightly Manic _____ Highly Manic _____

Angry _____ Anxious/fearful _____ Joyful _____ Hopeful _____

I woke up feeling rested today _____

Gratitude for today _____

I noticed the following emotions, body sensations, and thoughts *before* **the session** (list below):

Affirmation Group (if choosing a group): _____

After the session I noticed (place an X beside each YES answer):

_____ I was relaxed _____ I felt positive about my experience

_____ I was agitated / anxious _____ One or more of the affirmations challenged me

(Optional) Each day you have the option to choose one affirmation from your list for in-depth work.
Affirmation _____

SUDS: Subjective Units of Distress
Rate your distress on a scale between 0 (low) and 10 (high). Aim to achieve an ending SUDS of 2 or below.

Beginning **SUDS** level _____ Ending **SUDS** level _____

I notice that my daily sessions are creating positive changes (place an X beside each YES answer):

_____ in my relationship with others _____ in my relationship with myself

_____ in my self-care program _____ in my perception of my health / wellness

_____ in my ability to work through challenging issues and emotions

_____ in my confidence level and my feelings of self-worth

_____ in my daily activity level _____ in my perception of personal safety

_____ in my level of inner awareness _____ in my attitude toward life and its possibilities

_____ in my level of ability to grow and change

Other change _____

_____ Heart Massage

Week 8: I Choose a Joy-Filled Life

Then a woman said, Speak to us of Joy and Sorrow.
And he answered: Your joy is your sorrow unmasked.
~ Khalil Gibran

Program: Daily Meditations or work with an Affirmation List
If using Affirmations, create your list below:

This Week's Insights

Letting ourselves be forgiven is one of the most difficult healings we will undertake.
And one of the most fruitful.

~ Steven Levine

Self-Care First!

Positive emotional and physical self-care is the most beautiful gift that you can give to yourself and your family. Put a check beside the activity on the days you engage in it. Meditation, at least once each week, is part of the Nurturing Wellness Through Radical Self-Care Program. The other listed activities are optional. Yoga and Tai Chi are good for energy flow. Yoga is great for depression and Tai Chi is great support for trauma survivors. Consider making one or both of them part of your rejuvenation program.

Meditation: _____ _____ _____ _____ _____ _____ _____

Meditation Journal: _____ _____ _____ _____ _____ _____ _____

Walking Meditation: _____ _____ _____ _____ _____ _____ _____

Breathing Meditation: _____ _____ _____ _____ _____ _____ _____

Exercise Walk: _____ _____ _____ _____ _____ _____ _____

Yoga: _____ _____ _____ _____ _____ _____ _____

Tai Chi: _____ _____ _____ _____ _____ _____ _____

Bubble Bath / Hot Tub: _____ _____ _____ _____ _____ _____ _____

Gym Workout: _____ _____ _____ _____ _____ _____ _____

Running or Jogging: _____ _____ _____ _____ _____ _____ _____

Team or Partner Sports: _____ _____ _____ _____ _____ _____ _____

Swimming: _____ _____ _____ _____ _____ _____ _____

Aerobics Class: _____ _____ _____ _____ _____ _____ _____

Massage and Body Work / Energy Healing: _____ _____ _____ _____ _____ _____ _____

Manicure or Pedicure: _____

Other: (List the activity or exercise below):

_____: _____ _____ _____ _____ _____ _____ _____

_____: _____ _____ _____ _____ _____ _____ _____

_____: _____ _____ _____ _____ _____ _____ _____

Nurturing Wellness Journal Page

Day # _____   **Desired Outcome** _____

My Mood today is (check all that apply):

Good _____	Flat (Blah) _____	Depressed _____	Very depressed _____
Content _____	Erratic _____	Slightly Manic _____	Highly Manic _____
Angry _____	Anxious/fearful _____	Joyful _____	Hopeful _____

I woke up feeling rested today   _____

Gratitude for today _____

I noticed the following emotions, body sensations, and thoughts *before* **the session** (list below):

Affirmation Group (if choosing a group): _____

After the session I noticed (place an X beside each YES answer):

_____   I was relaxed   _____   I felt positive about my experience

_____   I was agitated / anxious   _____   One or more of the affirmations challenged me

(Optional) Each day you have the option to choose one affirmation from your list for in-depth work.
Affirmation _____

SUDS: Subjective Units of Distress
Rate your distress on a scale between 0 (low) and 10 (high). Aim to achieve an ending SUDS of 2 or below.

Beginning **SUDS** level _____   Ending **SUDS** level _____

I notice that my daily sessions are creating positive changes (place an X beside each YES answer):

_____ in my relationship with others   _____ in my relationship with myself

_____ in my self-care program   _____ in my perception of my health / wellness

_____ in my ability to work through challenging issues and emotions

_____ in my confidence level and my feelings of self-worth

_____ in my daily activity level   _____ in my perception of personal safety

_____ in my level of inner awareness   _____ in my attitude toward life and its possibilities

_____ in my level of ability to grow and change

Other change _____

_____   Heart Massage

Nurturing Wellness Journal Page

Day # _____ **Desired Outcome** _____

My Mood today is (check all that apply):

Good _____	Flat (Blah) _____	Depressed _____	Very depressed _____
Content _____	Erratic _____	Slightly Manic _____	Highly Manic _____
Angry _____	Anxious/fearful _____	Joyful _____	Hopeful _____

I woke up feeling rested today _____

Gratitude for today _____

I noticed the following emotions, body sensations, and thoughts *before* the session (list below):

Affirmation Group (if choosing a group): _____

After the session I noticed (place an X beside each YES answer):

_____ I was relaxed   _____ I felt positive about my experience

_____ I was agitated / anxious   _____ One or more of the affirmations challenged me

(Optional) Each day you have the option to choose one affirmation from your list for in-depth work.
Affirmation _____

SUDS: Subjective Units of Distress
Rate your distress on a scale between 0 (low) and 10 (high). Aim to achieve an ending SUDS of 2 or below.

Beginning **SUDS** level _____   Ending **SUDS** level _____

I notice that my daily sessions are creating positive changes (place an X beside each YES answer):

_____ in my relationship with others   _____ in my relationship with myself

_____ in my self-care program   _____ in my perception of my health / wellness

_____ in my ability to work through challenging issues and emotions

_____ in my confidence level and my feelings of self-worth

_____ in my daily activity level   _____ in my perception of personal safety

_____ in my level of inner awareness   _____ in my attitude toward life and its possibilities

_____ in my level of ability to grow and change

Other change _____

_____ Heart Massage

Nurturing Wellness Journal Page

Day # _____ Desired Outcome _____

My Mood today is (check all that apply):

Good _____	Flat (Blah) _____	Depressed _____	Very depressed _____
Content _____	Erratic _____	Slightly Manic _____	Highly Manic _____
Angry _____	Anxious/fearful _____	Joyful _____	Hopeful _____

I woke up feeling rested today   _____

Gratitude for today _____

I noticed the following emotions, body sensations, and thoughts *before* **the session** (list below):

Affirmation Group (if choosing a group): _____

After the session I noticed (place an X beside each YES answer):

_____ I was relaxed   _____ I felt positive about my experience

_____ I was agitated / anxious   _____ One or more of the affirmations challenged me

(Optional) Each day you have the option to choose one affirmation from your list for in-depth work.
Affirmation _____

SUDS: Subjective Units of Distress
Rate your distress on a scale between 0 (low) and 10 (high). Aim to achieve an ending SUDS of 2 or below.

Beginning **SUDS** level _____   Ending **SUDS** level _____

I notice that my daily sessions are creating positive changes (place an X beside each YES answer):

_____ in my relationship with others   _____ in my relationship with myself

_____ in my self-care program   _____ in my perception of my health / wellness

_____ in my ability to work through challenging issues and emotions

_____ in my confidence level and my feelings of self-worth

_____ in my daily activity level   _____ in my perception of personal safety

_____ in my level of inner awareness   _____ in my attitude toward life and its possibilities

_____ in my level of ability to grow and change

Other change _____

_____ Heart Massage

Nurturing Wellness Journal Page

Day # _____ **Desired Outcome** _____

My Mood today is (check all that apply):

Good _____	Flat (Blah) _____	Depressed _____	Very depressed _____
Content _____	Erratic _____	Slightly Manic _____	Highly Manic _____
Angry _____	Anxious/fearful _____	Joyful _____	Hopeful _____

I woke up feeling rested today _____

Gratitude for today _____

I noticed the following emotions, body sensations, and thoughts *before* the session (list below):

Affirmation Group (if choosing a group): _____

After the session I noticed (place an X beside each YES answer):

_____ I was relaxed _____ I felt positive about my experience

_____ I was agitated / anxious _____ One or more of the affirmations challenged me

(Optional) Each day you have the option to choose one affirmation from your list for in-depth work.
Affirmation _____

SUDS: Subjective Units of Distress
Rate your distress on a scale between 0 (low) and 10 (high). Aim to achieve an ending SUDS of 2 or below.

Beginning **SUDS** level _____ Ending **SUDS** level _____

I notice that my daily sessions are creating positive changes (place an X beside each YES answer):

_____ in my relationship with others _____ in my relationship with myself
_____ in my self-care program _____ in my perception of my health / wellness
_____ in my ability to work through challenging issues and emotions
_____ in my confidence level and my feelings of self-worth
_____ in my daily activity level _____ in my perception of personal safety
_____ in my level of inner awareness _____ in my attitude toward life and its possibilities
_____ in my level of ability to grow and change

Other change _____

_____ Heart Massage

Nurturing Wellness Journal Page

Day # _____ **Desired Outcome** _____

My Mood today is (check all that apply):

Good _____	Flat (Blah) _____	Depressed _____	Very depressed _____
Content _____	Erratic _____	Slightly Manic _____	Highly Manic _____
Angry _____	Anxious/fearful _____	Joyful _____	Hopeful _____

I woke up feeling rested today _____

Gratitude for today _____

I noticed the following emotions, body sensations, and thoughts *before* the session (list below):

Affirmation Group (if choosing a group): _____

After the session I noticed (place an X beside each YES answer):

_____ I was relaxed   _____ I felt positive about my experience

_____ I was agitated / anxious   _____ One or more of the affirmations challenged me

(Optional) Each day you have the option to choose one affirmation from your list for in-depth work.
Affirmation _____

SUDS: Subjective Units of Distress
Rate your distress on a scale between 0 (low) and 10 (high). Aim to achieve an ending SUDS of 2 or below.

Beginning **SUDS** level _____   Ending **SUDS** level _____

I notice that my daily sessions are creating positive changes (place an X beside each YES answer):

_____ in my relationship with others   _____ in my relationship with myself

_____ in my self-care program   _____ in my perception of my health / wellness

_____ in my ability to work through challenging issues and emotions

_____ in my confidence level and my feelings of self-worth

_____ in my daily activity level   _____ in my perception of personal safety

_____ in my level of inner awareness   _____ in my attitude toward life and its possibilities

_____ in my level of ability to grow and change

Other change _____

_____ Heart Massage

Week 9: Live a Peaceful Life

I come into the presence of still water.
And I feel above me the day-blind stars
Waiting with their light. For a time
I rest in the grace of the world, and am free.
~ Wendell Berry

Program: Daily Meditations or work with an Affirmation List
If using Affirmations, create your list below:

This Week's Insights

Knowledge of what is possible is the beginning of happiness.
~ George Santayana

Self-Care First!

Positive emotional and physical self-care is the most beautiful gift that you can give to yourself and your family. Put a check beside the activity on the days you engage in it. Meditation, at least once each week, is part of the Nurturing Wellness Through Radical Self-Care Program. The other listed activities are optional. Yoga and Tai Chi are good for energy flow. Yoga is great for depression and Tai Chi is great support for trauma survivors. Consider making one or both of them part of your rejuvenation program.

Meditation: ＿＿ ＿＿ ＿＿ ＿＿ ＿＿ ＿＿ ＿＿

Meditation Journal: ＿＿ ＿＿ ＿＿ ＿＿ ＿＿ ＿＿ ＿＿

Walking Meditation: ＿＿ ＿＿ ＿＿ ＿＿ ＿＿ ＿＿ ＿＿

Breathing Meditation: ＿＿ ＿＿ ＿＿ ＿＿ ＿＿ ＿＿ ＿＿

Exercise Walk: ＿＿ ＿＿ ＿＿ ＿＿ ＿＿ ＿＿ ＿＿

Yoga: ＿＿ ＿＿ ＿＿ ＿＿ ＿＿ ＿＿ ＿＿

Tai Chi: ＿＿ ＿＿ ＿＿ ＿＿ ＿＿ ＿＿ ＿＿

Bubble Bath / Hot Tub: ＿＿ ＿＿ ＿＿ ＿＿ ＿＿ ＿＿ ＿＿

Gym Workout: ＿＿ ＿＿ ＿＿ ＿＿ ＿＿ ＿＿ ＿＿

Running or Jogging: ＿＿ ＿＿ ＿＿ ＿＿ ＿＿ ＿＿ ＿＿

Team or Partner Sports: ＿＿ ＿＿ ＿＿ ＿＿ ＿＿ ＿＿ ＿＿

Swimming: ＿＿ ＿＿ ＿＿ ＿＿ ＿＿ ＿＿ ＿＿

Aerobics Class: ＿＿ ＿＿ ＿＿ ＿＿ ＿＿ ＿＿ ＿＿

Massage and Body Work / Energy Healing: ＿＿ ＿＿ ＿＿ ＿＿ ＿＿ ＿＿ ＿＿

Manicure or Pedicure: ＿＿

Other: (List the activity or exercise below):

＿＿＿＿＿＿＿＿＿＿＿＿＿ : ＿＿ ＿＿ ＿＿ ＿＿ ＿＿ ＿＿ ＿＿

＿＿＿＿＿＿＿＿＿＿＿＿＿ : ＿＿ ＿＿ ＿＿ ＿＿ ＿＿ ＿＿ ＿＿

＿＿＿＿＿＿＿＿＿＿＿＿＿ : ＿＿ ＿＿ ＿＿ ＿＿ ＿＿ ＿＿ ＿＿

Nurturing Wellness Journal Page

Day # _____ **Desired Outcome** _____

My Mood today is (check all that apply):

Good	_____	Flat (Blah)	_____	Depressed	_____	Very depressed	_____
Content	_____	Erratic	_____	Slightly Manic	_____	Highly Manic	_____
Angry	_____	Anxious/fearful	_____	Joyful	_____	Hopeful	_____

I woke up feeling rested today _____

Gratitude for today _____

I noticed the following emotions, body sensations, and thoughts *before* **the session** (list below):

Affirmation Group (if choosing a group): _____

After the session I noticed (place an X beside each YES answer):

_____ I was relaxed   _____ I felt positive about my experience

_____ I was agitated / anxious   _____ One or more of the affirmations challenged me

(Optional) Each day you have the option to choose one affirmation from your list for in-depth work.
Affirmation _____

SUDS: Subjective Units of Distress
Rate your distress on a scale between 0 (low) and 10 (high). Aim to achieve an ending SUDS of 2 or below.

Beginning **SUDS** level _____   Ending **SUDS** level _____

I notice that my daily sessions are creating positive changes (place an X beside each YES answer):

_____ in my relationship with others   _____ in my relationship with myself

_____ in my self-care program   _____ in my perception of my health / wellness

_____ in my ability to work through challenging issues and emotions

_____ in my confidence level and my feelings of self-worth

_____ in my daily activity level   _____ in my perception of personal safety

_____ in my level of inner awareness   _____ in my attitude toward life and its possibilities

_____ in my level of ability to grow and change

Other change _____

_____ Heart Massage

Nurturing Wellness Journal Page

Day # _____ **Desired Outcome** _____

My Mood today is (check all that apply):

Good	_____	Flat (Blah)	_____	Depressed	_____	Very depressed	_____
Content	_____	Erratic	_____	Slightly Manic	_____	Highly Manic	_____
Angry	_____	Anxious/fearful	_____	Joyful	_____	Hopeful	_____

I woke up feeling rested today _____

Gratitude for today _____

I noticed the following emotions, body sensations, and thoughts *before* the session (list below):

Affirmation Group (if choosing a group): _____

After the session I noticed (place an X beside each YES answer):

_____ I was relaxed   _____ I felt positive about my experience

_____ I was agitated / anxious   _____ One or more of the affirmations challenged me

(Optional) Each day you have the option to choose one affirmation from your list for in-depth work.
Affirmation _____

SUDS: Subjective Units of Distress
Rate your distress on a scale between 0 (low) and 10 (high). Aim to achieve an ending SUDS of 2 or below.

Beginning **SUDS** level _____   Ending **SUDS** level _____

I notice that my daily sessions are creating positive changes (place an X beside each YES answer):

_____ in my relationship with others   _____ in my relationship with myself

_____ in my self-care program   _____ in my perception of my health / wellness

_____ in my ability to work through challenging issues and emotions

_____ in my confidence level and my feelings of self-worth

_____ in my daily activity level   _____ in my perception of personal safety

_____ in my level of inner awareness   _____ in my attitude toward life and its possibilities

_____ in my level of ability to grow and change

Other change _____

_____ Heart Massage

Nurturing Wellness Journal Page

Day # _____   **Desired Outcome** _____

My Mood today is (check all that apply):

Good _____	Flat (Blah) _____	Depressed _____	Very depressed _____
Content _____	Erratic _____	Slightly Manic _____	Highly Manic _____
Angry _____	Anxious/fearful _____	Joyful _____	Hopeful _____

I woke up feeling rested today   _____

Gratitude for today _____

I noticed the following emotions, body sensations, and thoughts *before* the session (list below):

Affirmation Group (if choosing a group): _____

After the session I noticed (place an X beside each YES answer):

_____ I was relaxed   _____ I felt positive about my experience

_____ I was agitated / anxious   _____ One or more of the affirmations challenged me

(Optional) Each day you have the option to choose one affirmation from your list for in-depth work.
Affirmation _____

SUDS: Subjective Units of Distress
Rate your distress on a scale between 0 (low) and 10 (high). Aim to achieve an ending SUDS of 2 or below.

Beginning **SUDS** level _____   Ending **SUDS** level _____

I notice that my daily sessions are creating positive changes (place an X beside each YES answer):

_____ in my relationship with others   _____ in my relationship with myself
_____ in my self-care program   _____ in my perception of my health / wellness
_____ in my ability to work through challenging issues and emotions
_____ in my confidence level and my feelings of self-worth
_____ in my daily activity level   _____ in my perception of personal safety
_____ in my level of inner awareness   _____ in my attitude toward life and its possibilities
_____ in my level of ability to grow and change

Other change _____

_____ Heart Massage

Nurturing Wellness Journal Page

Day # _____   **Desired Outcome** _____

My Mood today is (check all that apply):

Good _____	Flat (Blah) _____	Depressed _____	Very depressed _____
Content _____	Erratic _____	Slightly Manic _____	Highly Manic _____
Angry _____	Anxious/fearful _____	Joyful _____	Hopeful _____

I woke up feeling rested today   _____

Gratitude for today _____

I noticed the following emotions, body sensations, and thoughts *before* **the session** (list below):

Affirmation Group (if choosing a group): _____

After the session I noticed (place an X beside each YES answer):

_____ I was relaxed   _____ I felt positive about my experience

_____ I was agitated / anxious   _____ One or more of the affirmations challenged me

(Optional) Each day you have the option to choose one affirmation from your list for in-depth work.
Affirmation _____

SUDS: Subjective Units of Distress
Rate your distress on a scale between 0 (low) and 10 (high). Aim to achieve an ending SUDS of 2 or below.

Beginning **SUDS** level _____   Ending **SUDS** level _____

I notice that my daily sessions are creating positive changes (place an X beside each YES answer):

_____ in my relationship with others   _____ in my relationship with myself

_____ in my self-care program   _____ in my perception of my health / wellness

_____ in my ability to work through challenging issues and emotions

_____ in my confidence level and my feelings of self-worth

_____ in my daily activity level   _____ in my perception of personal safety

_____ in my level of inner awareness   _____ in my attitude toward life and its possibilities

_____ in my level of ability to grow and change

Other change _____

_____ Heart Massage

Nurturing Wellness Journal Page

Day # _____ **Desired Outcome** _____

My Mood today is (check all that apply):

Good _____	Flat (Blah) _____	Depressed _____	Very depressed _____
Content _____	Erratic _____	Slightly Manic _____	Highly Manic _____
Angry _____	Anxious/fearful _____	Joyful _____	Hopeful _____

I woke up feeling rested today _____

Gratitude for today _____

I noticed the following emotions, body sensations, and thoughts *before* the session (list below):

Affirmation Group (if choosing a group): _____

After the session I noticed (place an X beside each YES answer):

_____ I was relaxed _____ I felt positive about my experience

_____ I was agitated / anxious _____ One or more of the affirmations challenged me

(Optional) Each day you have the option to choose one affirmation from your list for in-depth work.
Affirmation _____

SUDS: Subjective Units of Distress
Rate your distress on a scale between 0 (low) and 10 (high). Aim to achieve an ending SUDS of 2 or below.

Beginning **SUDS** level _____ Ending **SUDS** level _____

I notice that my daily sessions are creating positive changes (place an X beside each YES answer):

_____ in my relationship with others _____ in my relationship with myself

_____ in my self-care program _____ in my perception of my health / wellness

_____ in my ability to work through challenging issues and emotions

_____ in my confidence level and my feelings of self-worth

_____ in my daily activity level _____ in my perception of personal safety

_____ in my level of inner awareness _____ in my attitude toward life and its possibilities

_____ in my level of ability to grow and change

Other change _____

_____ Heart Massage

Week 10: I Am Content

When you can think of yesterday without regret
And tomorrow without fear, you are near contentment.
~ Author Unknown

Program: Daily Meditations or work with an Affirmation List
If using Affirmations, create your list below:

This Week's Insights

Your task is not to seek love, but merely to seek and find all the barriers within yourself that you have built against it.
~ Rumi

Self-Care First!

Positive emotional and physical self-care is the most beautiful gift that you can give to yourself and your family. Put a check beside the activity on the days you engage in it. Meditation, at least once each week, is part of the Nurturing Wellness Through Radical Self-Care Program. The other listed activities are optional. Yoga and Tai Chi are good for energy flow. Yoga is great for depression and Tai Chi is great support for trauma survivors. Consider making one or both of them part of your rejuvenation program.

Meditation: _____ _____ _____ _____ _____ _____ _____

Meditation Journal: _____ _____ _____ _____ _____ _____ _____

Walking Meditation: _____ _____ _____ _____ _____ _____ _____

Breathing Meditation: _____ _____ _____ _____ _____ _____ _____

Exercise Walk: _____ _____ _____ _____ _____ _____ _____

Yoga: _____ _____ _____ _____ _____ _____ _____

Tai Chi: _____ _____ _____ _____ _____ _____ _____

Bubble Bath / Hot Tub: _____ _____ _____ _____ _____ _____ _____

Gym Workout: _____ _____ _____ _____ _____ _____ _____

Running or Jogging: _____ _____ _____ _____ _____ _____ _____

Team or Partner Sports: _____ _____ _____ _____ _____ _____ _____

Swimming: _____ _____ _____ _____ _____ _____ _____

Aerobics Class: _____ _____ _____ _____ _____ _____ _____

Massage and Body Work / Energy Healing: _____ _____ _____ _____ _____ _____ _____

Manicure or Pedicure: _____

Other: (List the activity or exercise below):

_____: _____ _____ _____ _____ _____ _____ _____

_____: _____ _____ _____ _____ _____ _____ _____

_____: _____ _____ _____ _____ _____ _____ _____

Nurturing Wellness Journal Page

Day # _____   **Desired Outcome** _____

My Mood today is (check all that apply):

Good _____	Flat (Blah) _____	Depressed _____	Very depressed _____
Content _____	Erratic _____	Slightly Manic _____	Highly Manic _____
Angry _____	Anxious/fearful _____	Joyful _____	Hopeful _____

I woke up feeling rested today   _____

Gratitude for today _____

I noticed the following emotions, body sensations, and thoughts *before* **the session** (list below):

Affirmation Group (if choosing a group): _____

After the session I noticed (place an X beside each YES answer):

_____ I was relaxed   _____ I felt positive about my experience

_____ I was agitated / anxious   _____ One or more of the affirmations challenged me

(Optional) Each day you have the option to choose one affirmation from your list for in-depth work.
Affirmation _____

SUDS: Subjective Units of Distress
Rate your distress on a scale between 0 (low) and 10 (high). Aim to achieve an ending SUDS of 2 or below.

Beginning **SUDS** level _____   Ending **SUDS** level _____

I notice that my daily sessions are creating positive changes (place an X beside each YES answer):

_____ in my relationship with others   _____ in my relationship with myself

_____ in my self-care program   _____ in my perception of my health / wellness

_____ in my ability to work through challenging issues and emotions

_____ in my confidence level and my feelings of self-worth

_____ in my daily activity level   _____ in my perception of personal safety

_____ in my level of inner awareness   _____ in my attitude toward life and its possibilities

_____ in my level of ability to grow and change

Other change _____

_____ Heart Massage

Nurturing Wellness Journal Page

Day # _____   **Desired Outcome** _____

My Mood today is (check all that apply):

Good _____	Flat (Blah) _____	Depressed _____	Very depressed _____
Content _____	Erratic _____	Slightly Manic _____	Highly Manic _____
Angry _____	Anxious/fearful _____	Joyful _____	Hopeful _____

I woke up feeling rested today   _____

Gratitude for today _____

I noticed the following emotions, body sensations, and thoughts *before* **the session** (list below):

Affirmation Group (if choosing a group): _____

After the session I noticed (place an X beside each YES answer):

_____ I was relaxed   _____ I felt positive about my experience

_____ I was agitated / anxious   _____ One or more of the affirmations challenged me

---

(Optional) Each day you have the option to choose one affirmation from your list for in-depth work.
Affirmation _____

SUDS: Subjective Units of Distress
Rate your distress on a scale between 0 (low) and 10 (high). Aim to achieve an ending SUDS of 2 or below.

Beginning **SUDS** level _____   Ending **SUDS** level _____

I notice that my daily sessions are creating positive changes (place an X beside each YES answer):

_____ in my relationship with others   _____ in my relationship with myself
_____ in my self-care program   _____ in my perception of my health / wellness
_____ in my ability to work through challenging issues and emotions
_____ in my confidence level and my feelings of self-worth
_____ in my daily activity level   _____ in my perception of personal safety
_____ in my level of inner awareness   _____ in my attitude toward life and its possibilities
_____ in my level of ability to grow and change

Other change _____

_____ Heart Massage

Nurturing Wellness Journal Page

Day # _____ **Desired Outcome** _____

My Mood today is (check all that apply):

Good _____	Flat (Blah) _____	Depressed _____	Very depressed _____
Content _____	Erratic _____	Slightly Manic _____	Highly Manic _____
Angry _____	Anxious/fearful _____	Joyful _____	Hopeful _____

I woke up feeling rested today _____

Gratitude for today _____

I noticed the following emotions, body sensations, and thoughts *before* **the session** (list below):

Affirmation Group (if choosing a group): _____

After the session I noticed (place an X beside each YES answer):

_____ I was relaxed   _____ I felt positive about my experience

_____ I was agitated / anxious   _____ One or more of the affirmations challenged me

(Optional) Each day you have the option to choose one affirmation from your list for in-depth work.
Affirmation _____

SUDS: Subjective Units of Distress
Rate your distress on a scale between 0 (low) and 10 (high). Aim to achieve an ending SUDS of 2 or below.

Beginning **SUDS** level _____   Ending **SUDS** level _____

I notice that my daily sessions are creating positive changes (place an X beside each YES answer):

_____ in my relationship with others   _____ in my relationship with myself

_____ in my self-care program   _____ in my perception of my health / wellness

_____ in my ability to work through challenging issues and emotions

_____ in my confidence level and my feelings of self-worth

_____ in my daily activity level   _____ in my perception of personal safety

_____ in my level of inner awareness   _____ in my attitude toward life and its possibilities

_____ in my level of ability to grow and change

Other change _____

_____ Heart Massage

Nurturing Wellness Journal Page

Day # _____   **Desired Outcome** _____

My Mood today is (check all that apply):

Good _____	Flat (Blah) _____	Depressed _____	Very depressed _____
Content _____	Erratic _____	Slightly Manic _____	Highly Manic _____
Angry _____	Anxious/fearful _____	Joyful _____	Hopeful _____

I woke up feeling rested today _____

Gratitude for today _____

I noticed the following emotions, body sensations, and thoughts *before* **the session** (list below):

Affirmation Group (if choosing a group): _____

After the session I noticed (place an X beside each YES answer):

_____ I was relaxed   _____ I felt positive about my experience

_____ I was agitated / anxious   _____ One or more of the affirmations challenged me

(Optional) Each day you have the option to choose one affirmation from your list for in-depth work.
Affirmation _____

SUDS: Subjective Units of Distress
Rate your distress on a scale between 0 (low) and 10 (high). Aim to achieve an ending SUDS of 2 or below.

Beginning **SUDS** level _____   Ending **SUDS** level _____

I notice that my daily sessions are creating positive changes (place an X beside each YES answer):

_____ in my relationship with others   _____ in my relationship with myself

_____ in my self-care program   _____ in my perception of my health / wellness

_____ in my ability to work through challenging issues and emotions

_____ in my confidence level and my feelings of self-worth

_____ in my daily activity level   _____ in my perception of personal safety

_____ in my level of inner awareness   _____ in my attitude toward life and its possibilities

_____ in my level of ability to grow and change

Other change _____

_____ Heart Massage

Nurturing Wellness Journal Page

Day # _____ **Desired Outcome** _____

My Mood today is (check all that apply):

Good	_____	Flat (Blah)	_____	Depressed	_____	Very depressed	_____
Content	_____	Erratic	_____	Slightly Manic	_____	Highly Manic	_____
Angry	_____	Anxious/fearful	_____	Joyful	_____	Hopeful	_____

I woke up feeling rested today _____

Gratitude for today _____

I noticed the following emotions, body sensations, and thoughts *before* **the session** (list below):

Affirmation Group (if choosing a group): _____

After the session I noticed (place an X beside each YES answer):

_____ I was relaxed   _____ I felt positive about my experience

_____ I was agitated / anxious   _____ One or more of the affirmations challenged me

(Optional) Each day you have the option to choose one affirmation from your list for in-depth work.
Affirmation _____

SUDS: Subjective Units of Distress
Rate your distress on a scale between 0 (low) and 10 (high). Aim to achieve an ending SUDS of 2 or below.

Beginning **SUDS** level _____   Ending **SUDS** level _____

I notice that my daily sessions are creating positive changes (place an X beside each YES answer):

_____ in my relationship with others   _____ in my relationship with myself

_____ in my self-care program   _____ in my perception of my health / wellness

_____ in my ability to work through challenging issues and emotions

_____ in my confidence level and my feelings of self-worth

_____ in my daily activity level   _____ in my perception of personal safety

_____ in my level of inner awareness   _____ in my attitude toward life and its possibilities

_____ in my level of ability to grow and change

Other change _____

_____ Heart Massage

Week 11: I Am Divinely Made

And then the Lord God formed man from just the ground and breathed into his nostrils the breath of life: and man became a living being.
~ Genesis 2:7

Program: Daily Meditations or work with an Affirmation List
If using Affirmations, create your list below:

This Week's Insights

You are wholly complete, and your success in life will be in direct proportion to your ability to accept this truth about you.
~ Dr. Robert Anthony

Self-Care First!

Positive emotional and physical self-care is the most beautiful gift that you can give to yourself and your family. Put a check beside the activity on the days you engage in it. Meditation, at least once each week, is part of the Nurturing Wellness Through Radical Self-Care Program. The other listed activities are optional. Yoga and Tai Chi are good for energy flow. Yoga is great for depression and Tai Chi is great support for trauma survivors. Consider making one or both of them part of your rejuvenation program.

Meditation: _____ _____ _____ _____ _____ _____ _____

Meditation Journal: _____ _____ _____ _____ _____ _____ _____

Walking Meditation: _____ _____ _____ _____ _____ _____ _____

Breathing Meditation: _____ _____ _____ _____ _____ _____ _____

Exercise Walk: _____ _____ _____ _____ _____ _____ _____

Yoga: _____ _____ _____ _____ _____ _____ _____

Tai Chi: _____ _____ _____ _____ _____ _____ _____

Bubble Bath / Hot Tub: _____ _____ _____ _____ _____ _____ _____

Gym Workout: _____ _____ _____ _____ _____ _____ _____

Running or Jogging: _____ _____ _____ _____ _____ _____ _____

Team or Partner Sports: _____ _____ _____ _____ _____ _____ _____

Swimming: _____ _____ _____ _____ _____ _____ _____

Aerobics Class: _____ _____ _____ _____ _____ _____ _____

Massage and Body Work / Energy Healing: _____ _____ _____ _____ _____ _____ _____

Manicure or Pedicure: _____

Other: (List the activity or exercise below):

_____ : _____ _____ _____ _____ _____ _____ _____

_____ : _____ _____ _____ _____ _____ _____ _____

_____ : _____ _____ _____ _____ _____ _____ _____

Nurturing Wellness Journal Page

Day # _____   Desired Outcome _____

My Mood today is (check all that apply):

Good _____	Flat (Blah) _____	Depressed _____	Very depressed _____
Content _____	Erratic _____	Slightly Manic _____	Highly Manic _____
Angry _____	Anxious/fearful _____	Joyful _____	Hopeful _____

I woke up feeling rested today   _____

Gratitude for today _____

I noticed the following emotions, body sensations, and thoughts *before* the session (list below):

Affirmation Group (if choosing a group): _____

After the session I noticed (place an X beside each YES answer):

_____ I was relaxed   _____ I felt positive about my experience

_____ I was agitated / anxious   _____ One or more of the affirmations challenged me

(Optional) Each day you have the option to choose one affirmation from your list for in-depth work.
Affirmation _____

SUDS: Subjective Units of Distress
Rate your distress on a scale between 0 (low) and 10 (high). Aim to achieve an ending SUDS of 2 or below.

Beginning **SUDS** level _____   Ending **SUDS** level _____

I notice that my daily sessions are creating positive changes (place an X beside each YES answer):

_____ in my relationship with others   _____ in my relationship with myself

_____ in my self-care program   _____ in my perception of my health / wellness

_____ in my ability to work through challenging issues and emotions

_____ in my confidence level and my feelings of self-worth

_____ in my daily activity level   _____ in my perception of personal safety

_____ in my level of inner awareness   _____ in my attitude toward life and its possibilities

_____ in my level of ability to grow and change

Other change _____

_____ Heart Massage

Nurturing Wellness Journal Page

Day # _____ **Desired Outcome** _____

My Mood today is (check all that apply):

Good	_____	Flat (Blah)	_____	Depressed	_____	Very depressed	_____
Content	_____	Erratic	_____	Slightly Manic	_____	Highly Manic	_____
Angry	_____	Anxious/fearful	_____	Joyful	_____	Hopeful	_____

I woke up feeling rested today _____

Gratitude for today _____

I noticed the following emotions, body sensations, and thoughts *before* **the session** (list below):

Affirmation Group (if choosing a group): _____

After the session I noticed (place an X beside each YES answer):

_____ I was relaxed   _____ I felt positive about my experience

_____ I was agitated / anxious   _____ One or more of the affirmations challenged me

(Optional) Each day you have the option to choose one affirmation from your list for in-depth work.
Affirmation _____

SUDS: Subjective Units of Distress
Rate your distress on a scale between 0 (low) and 10 (high). Aim to achieve an ending SUDS of 2 or below.

Beginning **SUDS** level _____   Ending **SUDS** level _____

I notice that my daily sessions are creating positive changes (place an X beside each YES answer):

_____ in my relationship with others   _____ in my relationship with myself
_____ in my self-care program   _____ in my perception of my health / wellness
_____ in my ability to work through challenging issues and emotions
_____ in my confidence level and my feelings of self-worth
_____ in my daily activity level   _____ in my perception of personal safety
_____ in my level of inner awareness   _____ in my attitude toward life and its possibilities
_____ in my level of ability to grow and change

Other change _____

_____ Heart Massage

Nurturing Wellness Journal Page

Day # _____   Desired Outcome _____

My Mood today is (check all that apply):

Good _____	Flat (Blah) _____	Depressed _____	Very depressed _____
Content _____	Erratic _____	Slightly Manic _____	Highly Manic _____
Angry _____	Anxious/fearful _____	Joyful _____	Hopeful _____

I woke up feeling rested today   _____

Gratitude for today _____

I noticed the following emotions, body sensations, and thoughts *before* **the session** (list below):

Affirmation Group (if choosing a group): _____

After the session I noticed (place an X beside each YES answer):

_____ I was relaxed   _____ I felt positive about my experience

_____ I was agitated / anxious   _____ One or more of the affirmations challenged me

(Optional) Each day you have the option to choose one affirmation from your list for in-depth work.
Affirmation _____

SUDS: Subjective Units of Distress
Rate your distress on a scale between 0 (low) and 10 (high). Aim to achieve an ending SUDS of 2 or below.

Beginning **SUDS** level _____   Ending **SUDS** level _____

I notice that my daily sessions are creating positive changes (place an X beside each YES answer):

_____ in my relationship with others   _____ in my relationship with myself

_____ in my self-care program   _____ in my perception of my health / wellness

_____ in my ability to work through challenging issues and emotions

_____ in my confidence level and my feelings of self-worth

_____ in my daily activity level   _____ in my perception of personal safety

_____ in my level of inner awareness   _____ in my attitude toward life and its possibilities

_____ in my level of ability to grow and change

Other change _____

_____ Heart Massage

Nurturing Wellness Journal Page

Day # _____ **Desired Outcome** _____

My Mood today is (check all that apply):

Good _____	Flat (Blah) _____	Depressed _____	Very depressed _____
Content _____	Erratic _____	Slightly Manic _____	Highly Manic _____
Angry _____	Anxious/fearful _____	Joyful _____	Hopeful _____

I woke up feeling rested today   _____

Gratitude for today _____

I noticed the following emotions, body sensations, and thoughts *before* **the session** (list below):

Affirmation Group (if choosing a group): _____

After the session I noticed (place an X beside each YES answer):

_____ I was relaxed   _____ I felt positive about my experience

_____ I was agitated / anxious   _____ One or more of the affirmations challenged me

(Optional) Each day you have the option to choose one affirmation from your list for in-depth work.
Affirmation _____

SUDS: Subjective Units of Distress
Rate your distress on a scale between 0 (low) and 10 (high). Aim to achieve an ending SUDS of 2 or below.

Beginning **SUDS** level _____   Ending **SUDS** level _____

I notice that my daily sessions are creating positive changes (place an X beside each YES answer):

_____ in my relationship with others   _____ in my relationship with myself

_____ in my self-care program   _____ in my perception of my health / wellness

_____ in my ability to work through challenging issues and emotions

_____ in my confidence level and my feelings of self-worth

_____ in my daily activity level   _____ in my perception of personal safety

_____ in my level of inner awareness   _____ in my attitude toward life and its possibilities

_____ in my level of ability to grow and change

Other change _____

_____ Heart Massage

Nurturing Wellness Journal Page

Day # _____   **Desired Outcome** _____

My Mood today is (check all that apply):

Good _____	Flat (Blah) _____	Depressed _____	Very depressed _____
Content _____	Erratic _____	Slightly Manic _____	Highly Manic _____
Angry _____	Anxious/fearful _____	Joyful _____	Hopeful _____

I woke up feeling rested today _____

Gratitude for today _____

I noticed the following emotions, body sensations, and thoughts *before* **the session** (list below):

Affirmation Group (if choosing a group): _____

After the session I noticed (place an X beside each YES answer):

_____ I was relaxed   _____ I felt positive about my experience

_____ I was agitated / anxious   _____ One or more of the affirmations challenged me

(Optional) Each day you have the option to choose one affirmation from your list for in-depth work.
Affirmation _____

SUDS: Subjective Units of Distress
Rate your distress on a scale between 0 (low) and 10 (high). Aim to achieve an ending SUDS of 2 or below.

Beginning **SUDS** level _____   Ending **SUDS** level _____

I notice that my daily sessions are creating positive changes (place an X beside each YES answer):

_____ in my relationship with others   _____ in my relationship with myself

_____ in my self-care program   _____ in my perception of my health / wellness

_____ in my ability to work through challenging issues and emotions

_____ in my confidence level and my feelings of self-worth

_____ in my daily activity level   _____ in my perception of personal safety

_____ in my level of inner awareness   _____ in my attitude toward life and its possibilities

_____ in my level of ability to grow and change

Other change _____

_____ Heart Massage

Week 12: I Am Deserving of My Success

I truly believe that any man's finest hour, the greatest fulfillment of all he holds dear, is that moment when he has worked his heart out in a good cause and lies exhausted on the field of battle.
~ Vince Lombardi

Program: Daily Meditations or work with an Affirmation List
If using Affirmations, create your list below:

This Week's Insights

Your vision will become clear only when you look into your heart. Who looks outside, dreams. Who looks inside, awakens.
~ Carl Jung

Self-Care First!

Positive emotional and physical self-care is the most beautiful gift that you can give to yourself and your family. Put a check beside the activity on the days you engage in it. Meditation, at least once each week, is part of the Nurturing Wellness Through Radical Self-Care Program. The other listed activities are optional. Yoga and Tai Chi are good for energy flow. Yoga is great for depression and Tai Chi is great support for trauma survivors. Consider making one or both of them part of your rejuvenation program.

Meditation: ____ ____ ____ ____ ____ ____ ____

Meditation Journal: ____ ____ ____ ____ ____ ____ ____

Walking Meditation: ____ ____ ____ ____ ____ ____ ____

Breathing Meditation: ____ ____ ____ ____ ____ ____ ____

Exercise Walk: ____ ____ ____ ____ ____ ____ ____

Yoga: ____ ____ ____ ____ ____ ____ ____

Tai Chi: ____ ____ ____ ____ ____ ____ ____

Bubble Bath / Hot Tub: ____ ____ ____ ____ ____ ____ ____

Gym Workout: ____ ____ ____ ____ ____ ____ ____

Running or Jogging: ____ ____ ____ ____ ____ ____ ____

Team or Partner Sports: ____ ____ ____ ____ ____ ____ ____

Swimming: ____ ____ ____ ____ ____ ____ ____

Aerobics Class: ____ ____ ____ ____ ____ ____ ____

Massage and Body Work / Energy Healing: ____ ____ ____ ____ ____ ____ ____

Manicure or Pedicure: ____

Other: (List the activity or exercise below):

_____ : ____ ____ ____ ____ ____ ____ ____

_____ : ____ ____ ____ ____ ____ ____ ____

_____ : ____ ____ ____ ____ ____ ____ ____

Nurturing Wellness Journal Page

Day # _____   Desired Outcome _____

My Mood today is (check all that apply):

Good _____	Flat (Blah) _____	Depressed _____	Very depressed _____
Content _____	Erratic _____	Slightly Manic _____	Highly Manic _____
Angry _____	Anxious/fearful _____	Joyful _____	Hopeful _____

I woke up feeling rested today   _____

Gratitude for today _____

I noticed the following emotions, body sensations, and thoughts *before* the session (list below):

Affirmation Group (if choosing a group): _____

After the session I noticed (place an X beside each YES answer):

_____ I was relaxed   _____ I felt positive about my experience

_____ I was agitated / anxious   _____ One or more of the affirmations challenged me

(Optional) Each day you have the option to choose one affirmation from your list for in-depth work.
Affirmation _____

SUDS: Subjective Units of Distress
Rate your distress on a scale between 0 (low) and 10 (high). Aim to achieve an ending SUDS of 2 or below.

Beginning **SUDS** level _____   Ending **SUDS** level _____

I notice that my daily sessions are creating positive changes (place an X beside each YES answer):

_____ in my relationship with others   _____ in my relationship with myself

_____ in my self-care program   _____ in my perception of my health / wellness

_____ in my ability to work through challenging issues and emotions

_____ in my confidence level and my feelings of self-worth

_____ in my daily activity level   _____ in my perception of personal safety

_____ in my level of inner awareness   _____ in my attitude toward life and its possibilities

_____ in my level of ability to grow and change

Other change _____

_____ Heart Massage

Nurturing Wellness Journal Page

Day # _____   Desired Outcome _____

My Mood today is (check all that apply):

Good	_____	Flat (Blah)	_____	Depressed	_____	Very depressed	_____
Content	_____	Erratic	_____	Slightly Manic	_____	Highly Manic	_____
Angry	_____	Anxious/fearful	_____	Joyful	_____	Hopeful	_____

I woke up feeling rested today   _____

Gratitude for today _____

I noticed the following emotions, body sensations, and thoughts *before* the session (list below):

Affirmation Group (if choosing a group): _____

After the session I noticed (place an X beside each YES answer):

_____ I was relaxed   _____ I felt positive about my experience

_____ I was agitated / anxious   _____ One or more of the affirmations challenged me

(Optional) Each day you have the option to choose one affirmation from your list for in-depth work.
Affirmation _____

SUDS: Subjective Units of Distress
Rate your distress on a scale between 0 (low) and 10 (high). Aim to achieve an ending SUDS of 2 or below.

Beginning **SUDS** level _____   Ending **SUDS** level _____

I notice that my daily sessions are creating positive changes (place an X beside each YES answer):

_____ in my relationship with others   _____ in my relationship with myself
_____ in my self-care program   _____ in my perception of my health / wellness
_____ in my ability to work through challenging issues and emotions
_____ in my confidence level and my feelings of self-worth
_____ in my daily activity level   _____ in my perception of personal safety
_____ in my level of inner awareness   _____ in my attitude toward life and its possibilities
_____ in my level of ability to grow and change

Other change _____

_____ Heart Massage

Nurturing Wellness Journal Page

Day # _____   Desired Outcome _____

My Mood today is (check all that apply):

Good _____	Flat (Blah) _____	Depressed _____	Very depressed _____
Content _____	Erratic _____	Slightly Manic _____	Highly Manic _____
Angry _____	Anxious/fearful _____	Joyful _____	Hopeful _____

I woke up feeling rested today   _____

Gratitude for today _____

I noticed the following emotions, body sensations, and thoughts *before* **the session** (list below):

Affirmation Group (if choosing a group): _____

After the session I noticed (place an X beside each YES answer):

_____ I was relaxed   _____ I felt positive about my experience

_____ I was agitated / anxious   _____ One or more of the affirmations challenged me

(Optional) Each day you have the option to choose one affirmation from your list for in-depth work.
Affirmation _____

SUDS: Subjective Units of Distress
Rate your distress on a scale between 0 (low) and 10 (high). Aim to achieve an ending SUDS of 2 or below.

Beginning **SUDS** level _____   Ending **SUDS** level _____

I notice that my daily sessions are creating positive changes (place an X beside each YES answer):

_____ in my relationship with others   _____ in my relationship with myself

_____ in my self-care program   _____ in my perception of my health / wellness

_____ in my ability to work through challenging issues and emotions

_____ in my confidence level and my feelings of self-worth

_____ in my daily activity level   _____ in my perception of personal safety

_____ in my level of inner awareness   _____ in my attitude toward life and its possibilities

_____ in my level of ability to grow and change

Other change _____

_____ Heart Massage

Nurturing Wellness Journal Page

Day # _____ **Desired Outcome** _____

My Mood today is (check all that apply):

Good _____	Flat (Blah) _____	Depressed _____	Very depressed _____
Content _____	Erratic _____	Slightly Manic _____	Highly Manic _____
Angry _____	Anxious/fearful _____	Joyful _____	Hopeful _____

I woke up feeling rested today   _____

Gratitude for today _____

I noticed the following emotions, body sensations, and thoughts *before* **the session** (list below):

Affirmation Group (if choosing a group): _____

After the session I noticed (place an X beside each YES answer):

_____ I was relaxed   _____ I felt positive about my experience

_____ I was agitated / anxious   _____ One or more of the affirmations challenged me

(Optional) Each day you have the option to choose one affirmation from your list for in-depth work.
Affirmation _____

SUDS: Subjective Units of Distress
Rate your distress on a scale between 0 (low) and 10 (high). Aim to achieve an ending SUDS of 2 or below.

Beginning **SUDS** level _____   Ending **SUDS** level _____

I notice that my daily sessions are creating positive changes (place an X beside each YES answer):

_____ in my relationship with others   _____ in my relationship with myself

_____ in my self-care program   _____ in my perception of my health / wellness

_____ in my ability to work through challenging issues and emotions

_____ in my confidence level and my feelings of self-worth

_____ in my daily activity level   _____ in my perception of personal safety

_____ in my level of inner awareness   _____ in my attitude toward life and its possibilities

_____ in my level of ability to grow and change

Other change _____

_____ Heart Massage

Nurturing Wellness Journal Page

Day # _____   **Desired Outcome** _____

My Mood today is (check all that apply):

Good _____	Flat (Blah) _____	Depressed _____	Very depressed _____
Content _____	Erratic _____	Slightly Manic _____	Highly Manic _____
Angry _____	Anxious/fearful _____	Joyful _____	Hopeful _____

I woke up feeling rested today   _____

Gratitude for today _____

I noticed the following emotions, body sensations, and thoughts *before* the session (list below):

Affirmation Group (if choosing a group): _____

After the session I noticed (place an X beside each YES answer):

_____ I was relaxed   _____ I felt positive about my experience

_____ I was agitated / anxious   _____ One or more of the affirmations challenged me

(Optional) Each day you have the option to choose one affirmation from your list for in-depth work.
Affirmation _____

SUDS: Subjective Units of Distress
Rate your distress on a scale between 0 (low) and 10 (high). Aim to achieve an ending SUDS of 2 or below.

Beginning **SUDS** level _____   Ending **SUDS** level _____

I notice that my daily sessions are creating positive changes (place an X beside each YES answer):

_____ in my relationship with others   _____ in my relationship with myself

_____ in my self-care program   _____ in my perception of my health / wellness

_____ in my ability to work through challenging issues and emotions

_____ in my confidence level and my feelings of self-worth

_____ in my daily activity level   _____ in my perception of personal safety

_____ in my level of inner awareness   _____ in my attitude toward life and its possibilities

_____ in my level of ability to grow and change

Other change _____

_____ Heart Massage

Congratulations!

You have successfully completed your 12-week Nurturing Wellness Through Radical Self-Care Program.

Take a look at what you have accomplished!

You have increased your emotional self-care skills:
1. Balanced autonomic nervous system
2. Self acceptance
3. A balanced self-care routine
4. Awareness of personal gratitude and joy
5. Strategies for increasing positive thought
6. REB Posture and the Relaxation Response
7. REB and Affirmations for Emotional Release
8. Harmony Mind-Body Energetic Exercise
9. Mindful Meditation
10. Managing and releasing daily stressors
11. Daily inclusion of fun and laughter

You have become a healthier person through:
1. Now-focused living
2. Greater understanding of how to live a balanced life
3. Developing a mindfulness lifestyle
4. Increasing your personal awareness
5. Increased development of positive thought
6. Increased positive self-talk
7. Increasing self-knowledge
8. Participating in physical, emotional, and spiritual exercise
9. More fully embracing your personal power

You have improved your Spiritual Self-Care:
1. Recognition of the spiritual nature all of human beings
2. Acknowledging the possibility of personal spiritual communication
3. Increasing your self-awareness and self-insight
4. Understanding the very real connection between mind–body–spirit
5. Journaling
6. Meditation and deep relaxation
7. Embracing fun and laughter
8. Increasing positive thought
9. Connecting your Radiant Circuits through the REB posture

List the positive changes in your personal, family, spiritual, and work life:

1.
2.
3.
4.
5.
6.
7.
8.

REB SELF-CARE
for
LIFE

CHAPTER 8

Energetic Balancing with REB Self-Help Tools

Whether it be 'pranic' flows of the Chakra system, the 'chi' flows of the Acupuncture system, or the vibrational patterns of homeopathic nosodes, all energy medicines provide a mechanism of bringing informational energy into the physical body, and it is this informational energy that then sustains and maintains the physical body and its diverse physiological functions.
~ Phillip Warren

REB, Breath Work, and Sleep

Because REB relaxation is calming, it is a good sleep aid. If you rest quietly in the posture for 10–15 minutes prior to going to bed, your body and mind will be relaxed, your thoughts quieted. Personally I like to climb in bed and then hold the posture for a few moments so I can just drift off to sleep. If you have long-term sleep problems, try drinking some relaxing herbal tea blends prepared to aid sleep, and then spend some time in the posture. Think of it as REB and Tea Time. Some easy-to-find herbal tea blends that help with relaxation at bedtime are:

- Good Earth Tea for Sleep
- Yogi Bedtime Herbal Tea Supplement
- Celestial Seasonings Sleepytime
- Gaia Herbs Sleep & Relax Tea

The best tip I have about awakening during the night is to accept that you have awakened. Don't allow the sleeplessness to anger and frustrate you. The frustration, tossing, and turning only delay sleep and exhaust you. When you wake up in the middle of the night, REB will help you get back to sleep. I recommend that you find the easiest way to hold the posture comfortably while in bed. I usually turn on my side, because the bed helps support the posture. If no other health problems exist, once your relaxation response is locked in, sleep will be less of an issue or no issue at all.

A Breathing Tip

When stressed, we all take shallow breaths that deprive us of the oxygen our body needs causing greater physiological symptoms of stress. When we feel fearful, threatened in some way by our emotions or the events around us, we begin to breathe quickly and shallowly from high in our chest. This can lead to a full blown panic attack. "Normal deep breath" describes the kind of breath I'd like you to adopt. Normal breathing is belly breathing. Your abdomen rises and falls just like the belly of a sleeping baby. I suggest your *in* breath and *out* breath be nice and full, setting an intent to fill your lungs on each inhale and then empty them on each exhale. Please don't exaggerate your breath by huffing and puffing or forcefully blowing the exhale out your mouth. Breathe quietly through your nose. The ideal is a full, quiet *in* breath and a quiet peaceful *out* breath that occurs naturally when you are totally relaxed.

Breathing for Sleep

Remember the meditation Breathe, Imagine, Relax and Gap Breathing? We're going to incorporate Gap Breathing with Mindful Breathing. (Adding REB is an option.)

- Make sure you are in a sleeping position that you really like—a position that creates a cozy, relaxed feeling.
- Use the Gap Breathing you learned earlier. Begin by taking a nice, normal deep breath, hold it for a second and then drop the breath into your lower abdomen. Begin to breathe from your abdomen. Normal, deep breathing is calming.
- Breathe from your abdomen; inhale, continuing to use gap breathing.
- Begin to use the REB posture. Use bilateral squeezing if it is comforting to you. Bring the issue you are worrying about to mind and notice your body as you breathe. Notice the areas of bodily tension and focus on them as you breathe. You can imagine that you are breathing into the stressed areas. Continue focusing and breathing until the tension reduces or disappears. Notice the next area of tension and repeat the instructions. Notice your thoughts, especially worry and fear thoughts.
- Allow yourself to relax around each troubling thought until the emotional impact is gone.
- Focus on your breath. Notice yourself inhaling. Notice the quietness in the gap at the top of your inhale. Exhale, and notice the gap at the end of the exhale. Notice your body as you let go of stress with each exhale. Notice how it

feels to inhale, hold the gap, exhale, hold the gap. If you feel your mind begin to wonder, bring your focus back to the breath.

- Continue to breathe this way until you drift into sleep.
- If you haven't drifted off to sleep after a reasonable time, notice how relaxed your body has become. Continue to focus on your breath and your breathing. Resting quietly is much more preferable than tossing and turning or getting up and watching TV. Quiet rest is very deep and very restorative. Accept your situation and rest quietly.
- Occasionally I'll add paired words (peaceful–rest or soft–comforting) to my *in* breath and *out* breath in just the same way I add them during walking meditation. This causes a deep ANS response because you are getting the relaxation of the breath paired with the relaxing frequency of the verbal message.

REB and Medical Tests and Procedures

Evaluate your SUDS level just like you did when working with the affirmations. Ten means your stress is very high. Zero means your stress is resolved. Make note of your beginning SUDS level so you can monitor your progress. Getting your SUDS down to 2 should release most of your stress, but obviously a 0 is better.

As you prepare for your appointment, use REB to release your worries and fears. Choose a quiet space and give yourself enough time to sit in the posture and begin to relax. Notice what you are feeling emotionally and physically. As you think about your fear, begin the active release (bilateral squeezing or swaying) and continue until your body responds. You may feel the stressed areas move to a different location in your body or simply begin to lessen. If you started with shoulder stress and it moved to an aching stomach, simply notice the shift in the way your stress is expressing and allow your body to work through the symptoms. After you work with the physical symptoms, notice the emotional symptoms. If you still have negative thoughts and emotions, work on them in the same way you work with the physical symptoms. Stay with the process until you feel prepared for your appointment. It may take a little while, but I guarantee you, however long it takes, it is time well spent. You are in *re-training*, working toward a strong relaxation response!

When you arrive for your appointment, find a quiet spot in the waiting area and begin to hold the posture. The relaxation you obtain helps you cope with any last minute stress or fear. You can even take REB into the medical test or procedure if the medical equipment allows you to hold the posture. If you have progressed to the place where thinking of the posture causes immediate relaxation to occur, simply begin to think of the posture and you'll feel relaxed for the entire medical appointment.

REB works wonders in the dental chair for the fear of needles, fear of the drill, or any other fear or phobia that you experience at the dentist office. Clear up as much stress as you can prior to your appointment, then use the posture and the bilateral squeezing to release your fear and anxiety once you are in the office. When it is time to sit in the dental chair, begin to use the posture as soon as you sit down and continue holding the posture until your dental work is complete. You'll be amazed!

REB and Phobias

Phobias are thoroughly and efficiently cleared with REB, but it will take a little patience to work through all the physical and emotional symptoms. You may uncover an old event or issues that created the phobia. That event needs to be cleared as well as the symptoms you feel right now.

- Write down the phobia you want to clear. Create an intention for the session such as, "I choose to be completely over this XYZ phobia." If you have more than one phobia, work on one at a time.
- Determine your SUDS level so you can track your progress as you work through your issue.
- Engage the REB posture and wait for the first feelings of relaxation.
- Begin to use the bilateral squeezing or swaying and to observe the process from a witnessing point of view.
- Identify your areas of physical stress, one at a time, and work on them one at a time. For example, if your shoulders are aching, work with the bilateral squeezing or swaying from a witness perspective until your shoulders ease. Then move to the next area of stress and work on it in the same way until it, too, is relieved.
- Specific worries, emotions, or thoughts are treated exactly the same way as physical symptoms. Notice your thought and name it: worry, disgust, anger. Continue the bilateral squeezing or swaying as you observe yourself working through each negative thought or belief.
- If the memory of an event or incident comes to mind, honor it—even if you don't make the connection right away. *Your body has made the connection for you*. Continue to use active release until the emotions and associated areas of physical tension disappear.

REB and Panic Attacks

Panic attacks are terrifying. If you have panic attacks, fear is ruling your life. You develop fear of the panic, and fear becomes a way of life. It is a vicious cycle that can seem impossible to break. Anyone who has ever had a panic attack never wants to have a second one.

Medicine will stop panic attacks. However, medicine can't heal the underlying cause of the fear causing the imbalance in your system. Working through the underlying cause is your responsibility. Healing from panic is an inside job that is up to you, and saying it this bluntly is kind and compassionate. You have to do the work. You have to change your lifestyle, which might mean making changes in your diet.

If you have panic attacks, it is wise to restrict or stop the intake of caffeine, nicotine, and sugar products: coffee, caffeinated teas, chocolate, caffeinated soft drinks, cigarettes, cookies and cake, and all foods that cause you to have an allergic response. You may be able to add them back in small amounts once your ANS is balanced, but most likely you are going to have to limit or eliminate them from your diet. Diet change reduces your overall physical stress load, making panic less likely.

Beginning to meditate with REB may be slightly helpful if you don't make other changes, but you aren't going to have the results you desire. You don't have to make all the changes at once, but if you want the panic to end, you have to help your body–mind system with some conscientious self-care.

Here is the recipe for stopping a panic attack with REB. We talked about it earlier in the book, so you know how effective it is. You can feel calmer in less than a minute. It has near-100% success.

> *Teach this sequence to your spouse or other immediate family member. This person becomes your panic attack coach. Follow the directions below and remember to inhale and exhale through your nose in a nice, slow, and even rhythm. The in breath originates from your belly and prevents shallow chest breathing.*

- Sit in the REB posture and begin to relax. With intention, breathe in a steady, slow rhythm through your nose and from your belly.
- Begin the bilateral squeezing or swaying, remembering to breathe. The squeezing or swaying is nice and slow and rhythmic. The tendency is to sway and squeeze at a frantic pace. Slowing down supports the relaxation response.
- Have your helper begin to tap on the top of your head at your crown (where your soft spot was in infancy). Have him or her tap with the middle, pointer, and ring fingers. The tapping is light and rhythmic. Continue the tapping at the crown until the feeling of panic is gone.

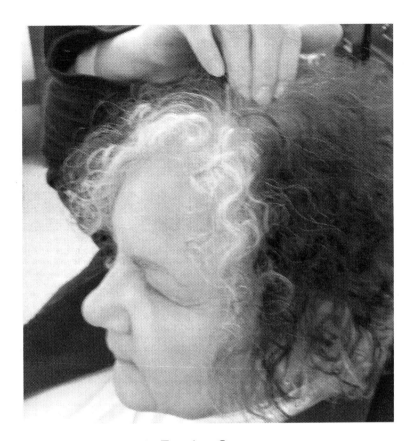

Tapping Crown

Photograph by Kirtan Coan

- If for some reason the bilateral squeezing or swaying, breathing, and tapping the crown do not immediately make a dramatic impact, the helper begins to tap the back of your neck, over the Bladder Meridians to quickly reduce fear. Have your helper lay his or her ring, middle, and pointer fingers across the back of your neck and begin to tap. Tap the area just above where your head and neck join, making sure to include both sides of your spinal column. Tapping the Bladder points at the back of the neck is the next step if tapping the crown does not ease your fear response.
- Confidently and calmly shift between tapping the crown and the Bladder meridian points at your neck. Do this until the panic stops.

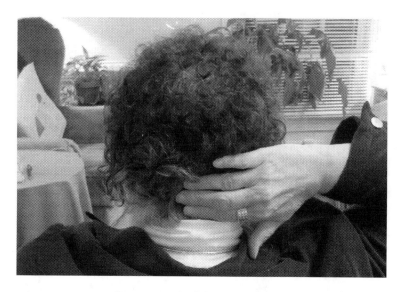

Tapping Bladder Meridians

Photo by Kirtan Coan

- Once the panic attack is over, continue to rest in the posture until your breathing is slow and even, and until you feel safe.
- The directions sound as though the process takes a long time. A panic attack usually ends very quickly.
- You can prevent a panic attack by beginning this process at the first sign an attack may be approaching. Learn to recognize the physical cues that alert you that anxiety is escalating.

Panic attacks that wake you up from a sound sleep can be the most startling. If you are alone, begin gap breathing and engage the REB posture and remain in it until you feel the first signs of relaxation begin. Release the posture and tap your crown 15 to 20 times. Engage the posture for a few breaths to deepen the response. Release the posture and tap the Bladder points at the back of your neck. Engage the posture for a few breaths and feel the relaxation. Continue this routine until your panic attack is gone.

Oasis

* * * * * *

My journey leads me home
To a place of peace and light.
A place within my heart
Of beauty and contentment.
A place where only love exists
And love becomes a way of life.

My loved ones are with me.
I trust them entirely.
I never hunger emotionally.
My innermost needs are met.
I am fully nurtured and blessed.
My Inner Shangri-la,
My oasis of peace and rest.

~ *Janet Gallagher Nestor*

PART 4

RESOURCES

and

REFERENCES

Appendix A: A List of Virtues—Aspects of Love

Abundance	Enliven	Honor	Patience	Strengthen
Acceptance	Equality	Hopefulness	Peacefulness	Supportive
Accomplishment	Excellence	Humility	Perceptiveness	Sureness
Accountability	Excitement	Humor	Playfulness	Sympathetic
Accuracy	Expansion	Important	Pleasure	Tactfulness
Achievement	Expressiveness	Inclusive	Poise	Teaching
Adaptability	Exuberance	Insight	Positivity	Tenacity
Agreeable	Faithfulness	Inspiration	Prayer	Tenderness
Alertness	Festive	Integration	Prayerful	Thoughtfulness
Assistance	Fitness	Integrity	Presence	Togetherness
Attuned	Flexible	Joy	Protect	Treasured
Balance	Focus	Kindness	Purity	Trust
Beauty	Forgiveness	Leadership	Quietness	Trustworthiness
Belief	Forthrightness	Limitlessness	Radiance	Truth
Calmness	Friendliness	Listen	Reconciliation	Truthfulness
Centered	Friendship	Love	Regard	Understanding
Choice	Generosity	Loyalty	Reflection	Unfailing
Clarity	Gentleness	Mastery	Relaxation	Unification
Comfort	Genuineness	Meaningfulness	Restfulness	Unity
Communication	Giving	Mercy	Responsiveness	Usefulness
Compassion	Gratefulness	Merriment	Reverence	Valor
Compromise	Gratitude	Mindfulness	Rootedness	Vibrancy
Concentration	Growth	Naturalness	Safety	Vigor
Consciousness	Guidance	Noticing	Service	Vitality
Courage	Hallowed	Nourishment	Silence	Virtuous
Creativity	Happiness	Nurturing	Simplicity	Warmth
Dependability	Harmony	Obedience	Sincerity	Wholeness
Devotion	Healing	Oneness	Smiling	Wisdom
Empathy	Health	Openness	Softness	Wise
Encouragement	Helpfulness	Opportunity	Solidarity	Working
Energetic	Holiness	Orderliness	Steadiness	Worthiness

This list is adapted from The List of Virtues that appears in *Pathways to Wholeness* by Janet Nestor (2010). I encourage you to meditate with the virtues that attract you. Engage the REB posture. When you feel yourself begin to relax, breathe in the chosen virtue and allow the energy to circulate through your body. Exhale all things inconsistent with the chosen virtue. Continue this way for several minutes until you can feel the essence of the virtue within.

Appendix B: A List of Feelings

We experience feelings in layers, not just one feeling at a time. In this chart the words are listed in alphabetical order for you to respond to, much like you would your own personal feelings. Which feelings are you comfortable with? Which ones create discomfort?

Accepted	Fascinated	Lucky	Skeptical
Abrupt	Fearful	Mad	Solid
Afraid	Festive	Miserable	Sorry
Alarmed	Forlorn	Melancholy	Spirited
Amazed	Free	Nervous	Surprised
Angry	Frightened	Nurturing	Tense
Ashamed	Frustrated	Offensive	Thankful
Aware	Glad	Optimistic	Thoughtful
Belligerent	Gleeful	Overjoyed	Threatened
Bitter	Gloomy	Overwhelmed	Timid
Bored	Grateful	Panicked	Tired
Brave	Grumpy	Peaceful	Tranquil
Carefree	Guilty	Positive	Trapped
Cheerful	Happy	Pessimistic	Trusted
Cheated	Helpless	Proud	Turbulent
Comfortable	Hesitant	Relaxed	Uneasy
Confident	Hopeful	Receptive	Understood
Confused	Hopeless	Regretful	Unloved
Considerate	Hostile	Reliable	Unwanted
Defeated	Hurt	Remorseful	Victimized
Delighted	Important	Resentful	Vicious
Depressed	Impulsive	Reserved	Vivacious
Detached	Irritated	Restless	Willing
Discouraged	Jealous	Resentful	Willful
Disgusted	Joyful	Sad	Withdrawn
Distressed	Jubilant	Secure	Wise
Empty	Kind	Sensitive	Worried
Encouraged	Lighthearted	Serene	Wronged
Excited	Lost	Shocked	Yearning

Glossary

Acute: An intense illness, trauma, or problem that is occurring now. *Acute pain. Acute illness. Acute panic attack.*

Addison's disease: Adrenal failure or severe adrenal insufficiency resulting from damage to the cortex of the adrenal glands. The damage can be caused by infections, autoimmune disease, hemorrhage, tumors, and blood-thinning medications. This disease affects men and women equally. Symptoms may include changes in heart rate and blood pressure, chronic diarrhea, darkening of the skin (patchy areas), paleness, extreme weakness and exhaustion, loss of appetite and unintended weight loss, nausea and vomiting, and salt craving.

Adrenal Fatigue: A less severe illness than Addison's disease that is often undiagnosed. It is a syndrome caused by the decreased ability of the adrenal glands to adapt to and respond adequately to stress. See http://www.adrenalfatigue.org, a website dedicated to people suffering from adrenal fatigue.

Autonomic Nervous System (ANS): A control system in charge of internal organs and glands, operates largely unconsciously to control heart rate, blood pressure, digestion, respiration rate, salivation, sexual arousal, perspiration, urination, and diameter of the pupils. The ANS has two branches: parasympathetic nervous system and sympathetic nervous system.

Bio-puncture: A process (or) the practice of injecting homeopathic medicines into acupoints in order to physiologically and energetically regulate the body. It treats pain, swelling, inflammation and toxin accumulation while boosting the immune system. The injections cause minor discomfort and their application is similar to the insertion of an acupuncture needle.

Central Vessel: Also called the Conception Vessel, this meridian regulates the yin energy in the body and controls the uterus and the embryo. The Conception Vessel runs along the body's front mid-line, flowing upward, from the pubic area to the lower lip. Along with the Governing Vessel, it does double-duty as part of the four Radiant Circuits.

Chronic: Long-lasting, usually longer than three months. It refers to a chronic human health problem or diseases like chronic fatigue syndrome, cancer, blindness, and heart disease. It also refers to mental health issues with residual symptoms. Post-traumatic stress disorder (PTSD) is an example of a chronic mental health issue.

Chronic Fatigue Syndrome: Ongoing, severe fatigue accompanied by a "fuzzy brain" sensation that feels much like a hangover or the flu. The symptoms come quickly and may be accompanied by reduced physical activity, muscle weakness, sore throat, cold symptoms, mild fever, tender lymph nodes, headache, severe stress, and depression.

Disordered Eating: Food, eating, and related body issues that do not rise to the level of a formal eating disorder diagnosis as defined in the Diagnostic and Statistical Manual of Mental Disorders. Individuals with disordered eating may exhibit serious food and body image symptoms and have symptoms of various diagnosable eating disorders.

Dysautonomia: The official name for severe malfunction or failure of the autonomic nervous system (ANS). Some researchers believe this condition to be beginning point of all illness because the ANS regulates all your organs, glands and primary bodily functions.

Electromagnetic Fields (EMFs): Invisible areas of energy extending from power lines, home electrical wiring, airport and military radar, transformers, computers, cell phones and cell phone towers, and appliances. Since the early-1980s, research has dramatically pointed out the dangers of EMFs although the results have been highly contested. The Environmental Protection Agency (EPA) warns "There is reason for concern" and advises "prudent avoidance" due to warnings about serious physical ailments possibly due to prolonged exposure. You can read more by exploring these sites: http://www.who.int/peh-emf/en/; http://www.bewholebewell.com/articles/GettingBuzzed.pdf; and http://brain101.info/EMF.php.

Emotional Self-Care: A self-help skill that includes emotional awareness and respect for your current, past, and future emotions. It encourages you to be aware of your emotional response, mindfully responding to them positively and in a clear, realistic manner. It includes eating when hungry, sleeping when tired, socializing with people you like and trust, living a now-oriented life, and seeking help when needed.

Energy Psychology: A family of techniques based on the acupoints of Chinese medicine and the chakras of Ayurvedic medicine. These comprehensive techniques are clinically observed to assist in the relief of many emotional-psychological conditions across a wide spectrum of symptoms. They are considered to be cutting-edge techniques and are compatible with talk therapy along with other forms of healing. Emotional Freedom Technique and Thought Field Therapy are two of the most widely known energy psychologies.

Fibromyalgia: A chronic condition that is often challenging to diagnose. It is usually associated with muscle pain occurring throughout the body and can often be identified by 18 tender points that cause pain when pressed. Fibromyalgia or Fibromyalgia Syndrome can be a primary illness or secondary to an underlying cause.

Fight or Flight or Fight-Flight-Freeze: A fundamental physiologic response that is wired into our mind–body connection and is the basis of today's stress medicine. It is our body's primitive, in-born process that prepares us for a perceived threat to our survival. The flight-or-fight response was discovered by American physiologist Walter Cannon.

Gap Breathing: This is a deep and meditative style of breathing that allows you to focus on the natural silence, the natural gap that occurs as you breathe. Inhale … gap, exhale … gap. Within the natural gap that occurs with every breath, there is complete silence—a place where you begin to know yourself and Creation.

Governing Vessel: Along with the Central Vessel, it is one of the two most important meridians in the human body. It performs double-duty as one of the four Radiant Circuits. The Governing Vessel begins at the base of the tail bone, runs up the spine, over the crown, and ends at the upper lip. It organizes the yang energy in the body.

Heart Rate Variability (HRV): A physiological phenomenon where the time intervals between heartbeats vary, and that variation is measured in microseconds. There is a great deal of scientific research supporting HRV as the best available predictor of illness and death. Variability (in the intervals between heartbeats) is the reflection of a healthy, well-developed autonomic nervous system. For good health indication these intervals should vary in what appears to be a random or chaotic fashion.

Institute of HeartMath: An internationally recognized research and educational organization dedicated to helping people reduce stress, regulate emotions, and live healthy, happy lives. It has developed sophisticated, cutting-edge technology to assist relaxation, helping individuals learn to rely on the intelligence that naturally exists within our physical hearts and minds. See www.hearthmath.org.

Meridians: There are twelve primary meridians that flow energy through the human body in the same way our veins flow blood through our body. The flow of energy through the meridians is as critical as the flow of blood through our veins. Both maintain life. The meridians affect every organ and system in the human body. Animals have meridians just as human beings do.

Microcosmic Orbit: Microcosmic Orbit is an ancient Taoist method of enhancing chi and circulating it throughout the body via the Governing and Central vessels (meridians). Simply explained, the circulation can be achieved with breath work or through visualization, or a combination of both. The chi is circulated in an arc beginning at your first chakra, up your back, along your spine, over your head (Governing Vessel), and down the mid-line of your body back to the starting place (Central Vessel).

Mindful Meditation: A type of meditation stemming from the Sanskrit idea of right-mindedness and from Buddhist Meditation. During mindful meditation you do not deny your thoughts but allow them to float in and out without attaching to them. In letting them float in and out, you are able to detach and relax deeply. Heightened awareness is a central aspect of this style of meditation.

Neuromuscular System: The muscles of the body and the nerves that supply them to produce coordination of functioning.

Parasympathetic Nervous System (PSNS): One of the two main branches of the autonomic nervous system, the PSNS regulates the rest-and-digest functions of the body that occur when an individual is relaxed and at rest. The PSNS works in unity with the sympathetic nervous system.

Peristalsis: The movement of the intestines caused by smooth muscle contractions. The movement pushes chyme (partially digested food) to move along the length of the intestine.

Porges' Smart Vagus: A part of the Social Engagement System that regulates the somatic muscles of speech and eating and is related to processes associated with attention, motion, emotion, and communication. It also regulates the heart and the bronchi to promote calm and self-soothing states.

Post-Traumatic Stress Disorder (PTSD): An anxiety disorder often diagnosed years after a trauma has occurred. It develops as a result of an unresolved traumatic experience: being in a severe automobile accident, being a combat soldier, being raped, being lost and alone, or witnessing a murder.

Progressive Relaxation or Progressive Muscle Relaxation (PMR): Developed by physician Edmund Jacobson in the 1920s with the intention of reducing muscle tension (anxiety) by tensing and releasing muscles. When engaging in Progressive Relaxation, you begin relaxing with the feet and legs and gradually move upward until all muscle groups are relaxed.

Primitive or Vegetative Vagus: Regulates smooth and cardiac muscles and is associated with passive reflexive regulation (actions that happen without our conscious assistance) of visceral change to bodily functions: Peristalsis of the GI tract, sweating, the action of the lungs, diaphragm, stomach. It is responsible for heart rate, dilation of blood vessels, and blood pressure. The most primitive function is the freeze response.

Psychological Reversal: Sometimes called a thought reversal, a psychological reversal represents a faulty, backwards thought process. An example of a psychological reversal is, "It is impossible for me to get over this problem." All problems are solvable by making an environmental change, a physical change, or by making an internal emotional shift that positively changes your mental–emotional approach to a problem.

Radiant Circuits: Defined by traditional Chinese medicine, the Radiant Circuits embody a distinct, spontaneous intelligence as they are able to help out where they are needed to revitalize, bring joy and spiritual connection into our lives. Four of our twelve meridians do double-duty as Radiant Circuits: the Triple Warmer and Spleen meridians, and the Central and Governing vessels.

Radiant Energies Balance (REB): An Energy Psychology that utilizes the Radiant Circuits to stimulate deep relaxation and the release of negative unwanted emotions and beliefs. It is exceptionally effective with all anxiety disorders, including phobias and panic disorders. REB is considered to be a viable alternative to Eye Movement Desensitization and Reprocessing (EMDR) in the treatment of trauma.

Rapid Cycling Bipolar Disorder: This term describes many different patterns of cycling between episodes of mania and depression. The patterns of cycles are not fixed and can change depending on factors including drinking alcohol, street drugs, stress, medical illness, medications, therapy, and positive support. The illness displays differently with each patient.

Somatic/Body Psychology: An interdisciplinary holistic approach to psychology. The word Somatic stems from the Greek word *soma* which means body. This approach dates back as far as Pierre Janet and was developed as a field within psychology by Wilhelm Reich. Somatic Psychology is very influential in the treatment of trauma. REB, EMDR, and Mindfulness are examples of Somatic Psychology as are all movement and dance therapies.

Somatic Sensory System: Provides sensory information for the nervous system. It is the part of the peripheral nervous system concerned with our sense of touch, pain, temperature, and kinesthesis.

Spiritual Self-Care: A concept involving the activities we engage in that help us find a positive sense of self and a sense of purpose and meaning in our daily lives. It is about developing compassion and love for ourselves and others, along with a connection to something greater than ourselves (God, Higher Power, Universal Flow, Creator of All).

Spleen Meridian: The Spleen/Pancreas meridian supports all the organs in the human body. It does double-duty as one of the four Radiant Circuits, is in charge of the body's rest-and-digest response, and governs the yin energy within the body. The Spleen meridian has strong nurturing qualities.

Sympathetic Nervous System (SNS): One of the two main branches of the autonomic nervous system, the SNS regulates the body's fight-or-flight response. The SNS mobilizes an individual in times of stress and danger.

Third Eye Chakra Center: Also known as the brow center and the mystical center of intuition. The front-body location is between the eyebrows, and the back-body location is at the base of the skull. The pineal and pituitary glands are associated with this chakra, as are the brain, eyes, ears, and nose.

Thought Chain (positive or negative): A positive thought chain is a series of thoughts, building upon one another, that create positive action and positive outcomes in your life. A negative thought chain is a series of negative thoughts that create negative actions and outcomes in your daily life.

Triple Warmer Meridian: This meridian is also known as the Triple Heater or Triple Burner. It is one of the four meridians performing double-duty as Radiant Circuits. It is responsible for the fight-or-flight response and pairs with the Spleen meridian to manage stress within your body.

The Origins of Radiant Energies Balance (REB)

by Phillip Warren

The following article was written by Phillip W. Warren, REB's originator and professor emeritus in psychology and music at Kwantlen Polytechnic University, Vancouver, British Columbia, Canada. It appears here with his permission and his blessing. All underlined words appear in the glossary, beginning on page 221.

This article provides a brief summary of the various aspects of the complete <u>Radiant Energies Balance (REB)</u> Protocol. Complex, multifaceted cases require a multi modal therapeutic approach. Trauma therapy research has demonstrated the inadequacy of pure talk/cognitive approaches which still seem the preferred modus operandi of most therapists (ref 1).

I became intrigued with the idea of using the acupuncture points of traditional Chinese medicine for psychological problems and began exploring their potency in the mid-1990s (ref 2). They worked amazingly well for simple delimited problems such as phobias (ref 3). However as I confronted more complex cases I realized that more sophisticated approaches were needed. Thus, I began my research to discover what these might be. I had been following the literature in trauma therapy and knew that their slogan "the body keeps the score" (ref 4) had to be part of the total approach. I also found the field of <u>somatic/body psychotherapy</u> provided powerful interventions (ref 5).

Research in the role of the eye movements and eye positions (ref 6), the role of body movement, stretching and the cerebellum in information processing (ref 7) indicated that these elements should be part of the total approach.

Research indicates that the two halves of the brain process emotional information differently (ref 8) and this must also be part of the overall approach.

An imbalance of the two branches of the <u>autonomic nervous system (sympathetic and parasympathetic)</u> (ref 9) is the source of many psychological problems and so I began my search for a non-invasive and efficient way to balance the autonomic nervous system (ANS). Especially vital in this balance activity is empowering <u>Porges' "Smart or Social Vagus"</u> so that the <u>"Primitive Vagus"</u> does not run amok and the Social Vagus can serve as a break on the sympathetic.

This non-invasive method I discovered in May 2001 where I had an epiphany: I discovered that Donna Eden's <u>Radiant Circuits</u> were the most efficient way to work with the body's energy system to balance the ANS and empower the "Smart or Social Vagus" (ref 10). According to Eden, the Radiant Circuits (or extraordinary meridians of traditional Chinese medicine) serve as "hot links" to the whole meridian system and, with focused intention, send corrective "active" information to where ever balance is needed.

Stimulating the mucosa of the nose also helps balance the ANS and so breathing through the nose is part of the protocol (ref 11).

One of the most effective indicators of the health of the ANS is the <u>Heart Rate Variability</u> (HRV) measure. This measure is used extensively by the <u>Institute of HeartMath</u> as biofeedback, so I incorporated in the protocol the very powerful and simple approaches from the Institute of HeartMath.

Their most recent approach involves the powerful concept of Coherence (ref 12). Mainstream psychology has largely neglected the importance of the heart in overall psychological well-being (ref 13).

Finally, in this summary I mention using the ancient tradition of "<u>mindful meditation</u>" where you assume a witnessing stance regarding symptoms (mental, emotional, and physical); this in itself is therapeutic (ref 14).

Beginning in 2001, Janet and I spent the next three years researching, developing, and refining the Radiant Energies Balance (REB) Protocol (http://REBprotocol.net). The protocol can be used on its own as a sophisticated professional therapeutic system but is also compatible with mainstream methods. The self-help version of the clinical protocol is available at http://www.rebprotocol.net/REB%20Self%20Help%20version%20Oct2005.pdf.

In sum, it is a unique and powerful, compact, and integrated blend of cutting-edge therapeutic methods from the cognitive, <u>somatic/body</u> and <u>energy/information psychotherapies</u>.

The rationale behind each of the aspects of the Radiant Energies Balance (REB)^{sm} Protocol are contained in the document on the website titled "An Active Ingredients Analysis of the Radiant Energies Balance Protocol" is available at: http://www.rebprotocol.net/Active2007.pdf. It provides a complete explanation of the many aspects built into the protocol which contribute to its power. For other information on research and evaluation of energy/information approaches see ref 15.

References for this article begin on page 229.

A complete developmental reference for the Radiant Energies Balance is available at http://www.rebprotocol.net.

References: Origins of Radiant Energies Balance / Phillip Warren

See http://ww.rebprotocol.net *for full list of developmental references.*

1. Wylie, M.S., (2004a) "The limits of talk: Bessel van der Kolk wants to transform the treatment of trauma," <u>Psychotherapy Networker</u>, v. 28, #1, January/February, 30-36, 38-41, 67. Available at http://www.traumacenter.org/products/pdf_files/Networker.pdf

    Wylie, M.S., (2004b) "Beyond talk: Using our bodies to get to the heart of the matter," <u>Psychotherapy Networker</u>, v. 28, #4, July/August, 24-28, 31-33. Available at http://www.bodymindtranquility.com/upload/Beyond%20Talk--Using%20Our%20Bodies.doc

2. Feinstein, D., (2003) "Subtle Energy: Psychology's missing link," <u>IONS Review</u>, Spring #64, 18-23, 35. Available at http://www.rebprotocol.net/IONSfeinstein.pdf

3. Feinstein, D., (2005a) "The latest insta-cure? Examining the controversy over energy psychology," <u>Psychotherapy Networker</u>, v. 29, #1, January/February, 77-83, 86-87. Revised version "Energy Psychology and the Instant Phobia Cure: New Paradigm or the Old Razzle Dazzle?" available at http://www.rebprotocol.net/phobiafeinstein.pdf

    Feinstein, D., (2010) "Rapid Treatment of PTSD: Why Psychological Exposure with Acupoint Tapping May Be Effective" <u>Psychotherapy: Theory, Research, Practice, Training</u>, v. 47(3), 385-402. Available at http://energypsyched.com/mechanisms.pdf

4. Rothschild, B., (2000) *The Body Remembers: The Psychophysiology of Trauma and Trauma Treatment,* W.W. Norton

    Scaer, R.C., (2001) *The Body Bears the Burden: Trauma, Dissociation, and Disease,* Haworth Press, Binghamton, NY

    van der Kolk, B.A. (1994) "The body keeps the score: Memory and the evolving psychobiology of post traumatic stress," <u>Harvard Review of Psychiatry</u>, v. 1, #5, 253-265. Available at http://www.trauma-pages.com/a/vanderk4.php

5. Johnson, D.H. and I.J. Grand, eds. (1998) *The Body in Psychotherapy: Inquiries in Somatic Psychology,* North Atlantic Books

    Ogden, P. and K. Minton (2000) "Sensory psychotherapy: One method for processing traumatic memory," <u>Traumatology</u>, v. 6, #3, Article 3, October. Available at www.fsu.edu/~trauma/v6i3/v6i3a3.html

Blakeslee, Sandra and Matthew Blakeslee (2007) *The Body Has a Mind of Its Own: How Body Maps in Your Brain Help you Do (Almost) Everything Better,* Random House

6. Hartung, J.G. and M.D. Galvin (2003) *Energy Psychology and EMDR: Combining Forces to Optimize Treatment,* W.W. Norton

Furman, M.E. and F.P. Gallo, (2000) *The Neurophysics of Human Behavior: Explorations at the Interface of Brain, Mind, Behavior, and Information,* CRC Press

Luer, G., U. Lass and J. Shallo-Hoffman, (1988) *Eye Movement Research: Physiological and Psychological Aspects,* Lewiston, NY, C.J. Hogrefe

Shapiro, Francine (1995) *Eye Movement Desensitization and Reprocessing: Basic Principles, Protocols, and Procedures,* The Guilford Press. EMDR Institute website http://www.emdr.com/

7. Oschman, J.L. (2000) *Energy Medicine: The Scientific Basis,* Churchill, Livingstone

Oschman, J.L. (2003) *Energy Medicine in Therapeutics and Human Performance,* Churchill, Livingstone

Schumahmann, J.D. (ed), (1997) <u>The Cerebellum and Cognition, International Review of Neurobiology</u>, v. 41, Academic Press

Leiner, H.C. and A.L. Leiner, (1997) "The treasure the bottom of the brain," (the cerebellum). Available at http://education.jhu.edu/newhorizons/Neurosciences/articles/-The%20Treasure%20at%20the%20Bottom%20of%20the%20Brain/index.html.

8. Schiffer, F., (1998) *Of Two Minds: The Revolutionary Science of Dual-Brain Psychology,* The Free Press

Schiffer, F., (2000) "Can the different cerebral hemispheres have distinct personalities? Evidence and its implications for theory and treatment of PTSD and other disorders," <u>Journal of Trauma and Dissociation</u>, v. 1, 83-104. Available at http://www.schiffermd.com/schiffermd.com/-Review_Article_on_Dual-Brain_Psychology.html.

Cook, A.C. and R. Bradshaw, (2002) <u>Toward Integration: One Eye at a Time</u>, SightPsych Seminars Incorporated, Vancouver, B.C.

9. Thayer, J.F., B.H. Friedman, and T.D. Borkovec (1996) "Autonomic characteristics of generalized anxiety disorder and worry," Biological Psychiatry, v. 39, 255-266

List of articles on Heart Rate Variability (HRV) and psychology available at http://www. atft.org/library/7-ArticlesHRVtoTFT.htm

Article on Heart Rate Variability (HRV) http://en.wikipedia.org/wiki/Heart_rate_ variability

Friedman, B., and F. Thayer, (1998a) "Autonomic balance revisited: Phobic anxiety and heart rate variability." Journal of Psychosomatic Research, v. 44(1), 133-151

Friedman, B., & J. Thayer, (1998b) "Anxiety and autonomic flexibility: A cardiovascular approach," Biological Psychology, v. 49 (3, Nov), 303-323

Hoenh-Saric, R. and D.R. McLeod, (1993) Biology of Anxiety Disorders, American Psychiatric Press

Porges, S.W. (1995) "Orienting in a defensive world: Mammalian modifications of our evolutionary heritage. A Polyvagal Theory," Psychophysiology, v. 32, 301-318. Available at www.wam.umd.edu/~sporges/polyvag.htm

Porges, S.W. (2001) "The polyvagal theory: Phylogenetic substrates of a social nervous system," International Journal of Psychophysiology, v. 42, 123-146

Porges, S.W. (2004) "Neuroception: A subconscious system for detecting threats and safety," Zero to Three, v. 24 #5, May, 19-24

10. Eden, D. with D. Feinstein (1993) Energy Medicine, Jeremy P. Tarcher/Putnam

See Eden and Feinstein web site: www.innersource.net

Eden, D. and D. Feinstein, (2002a) "Triple Warmer: It's Hotter Than You Think," Chap 8, 91-97 in Willem Lammers and Beate Kircher (Eds.) The Energy Odyssey: New Directions in Energy Psychology, Second, revised edition. Published by IAS Publications, Bahnhofstrasse 2, 7304 Maienfeld, Switzerland, Email: info@iasag.ch. Available at: http://www.rebprotocol.net/Triple%20Warmer-%20hotter%20than%20 you%20think.pdf

Eden, D. and D. Feinstein, (2002b) "Radiant Circuits: The Energies of Joy," in F.P Gallo (ed) *Energy Psychology in Psychotherapy: A Comprehensive Source Book,* New York: W. W. Norton, pp. 340-359

Feinstein, David, Donna Eden, and Gary Craig (2005) *The Promise of Energy Psychology: Revolutionary Tools for Dramatic Personal Change,* Jeremy P. Tarcher/ Putman. See website http://www.EnergyPsychEd.com

11. Shannahoff-Khalsa, D.S.,(2001/actual publication date 2002) "Unilateral Forced Nostril Breathing: Basic science, clinical trials, and selected advanced techniques," Subtle Energies and Energy Medicine, v. 12, #2, 79-106

Shannahoff-Khalsa, D.S., and L.R. Beckett, (1996) "Clinical; case report: Efficacy of yogic techniques in the treatment of obsessive compulsive disorders," International Journal of Neuroscience, v. 85, 1-17

12. Childre, D. and H. Martin, (1999) *The HeartMath Solution,* HarperSanFrancisco

Childre, D. and D. Rozman, (2002) *Overcoming Emotional Chaos,* Jodere Group

McCraty, R., M. Atkinson and D. Tomasino, (2001) Science of the Heart: Exploring the Role of the Heart in Human Performance: An Overview of Research Conducted by the Institute of HeartMath, Institute of HeartMath, Boulder Creek, CA. available at www. heartmath.org/research

Armour, J. Andrew (2003) Neurocardiology—Anatomical and Functional Principles, Institute of HeartMath, Boulder Creek, CA. available at www.heartmath.org/ research

McCraty, Rollin, Mike Atkinson, Dana Tomasino, and Raymond Trevor Bradley (2009) "The Coherent Heart: Heart–Brain Interactions, Psychophysiological Coherence, and the Emergence of System-Wide Order," Integral Review December v. 5, # 2, 10-115

McCraty, R., and Childre D. (2010) "Coherence: Bridging Personal, Social, & Global Health" *Alternative Therapies in Health and Medicine,* Jul/Aug, v. 16, # 4, 10-24

Ho, M-W (2006) "Quantum Jazz: The meaning of life, the universe and everything," Science in Society 32. http://www.i-sis.org.uk/isisnews/sis32.php

Ho, M-W (2007) "The Heartbeat of Health & Happiness Is A Heartbeat Away: Physics of Organisms & Applications" Institute of Science in Society, Press Releases 2007 July 25 & August 3.

http://www.i-sis.org.uk/HeartbeatofHealth.php

13. Pearsall, P. (1998) *The Heart's Code: Tapping the Wisdom and Power of Our Heart Energy,* Broadway Books

14. Harris, Bill, (2003) "Resistance—and Focusing on What You Don't Want: Birds of a Feather," <u>Mind Chatter</u> #127 (Interim Report) 2003 December 1 available at https://www.centerpointe.com/newsletter/edition_127.php#start

Paul Fulton, *The Institute for Meditation and Psychotherapy (IMP)* is dedicated to the training of mental health professionals interested in the integration of mindfulness meditation and psychotherapy. 35 Pleasant Street, Newton, Massachusetts 02459. Website: http://www.meditationandpsychotherapy.org/

For research updates on the use of mindfulness approaches in psychology see http://www.mindfulexperience.org/

15. Research summaries and overviews available at:

Feinstein, D., (2005b) "An overview of research in energy psychology," available at http://www.rebprotocol.net/overviewfeinstein.pdf and

http://energypsych.org/displaycommon.cfm?an=5 and

http://www.innersource.net/ep/component/content/article/75.html

Feinstein, D. "The Neurological Foundations of Energy Psychology, Brain Scan Changes During 4 Weeks of Treatment for Generalized Anxiety Disorder" available at http://www.innersource.net/ep/articlespublished/neurological-foundations.html

Gallo, F (2005) *Energy Psychology,* 2nd edition, CRC Press. A comprehensive overview of the field of energy/information psychology and psychotherapy

Church, Dawson (2007) *The Genie in Your Genes: Epigenetic Medicine and the New Biology of Intention,* Elite Books. Website http://www.dawsonchurch.com/ for an overview of recent research on the biological/genetic expression impact of energy/information psychology

References: Nurturing Wellness Through Radical Self-Care

Energy Psychology – Energy Medicine References

Meridians and Emotions
John Diamond, MD
www.drjohndiamond.com

Energy Medicine
Donna Eden and David Feinstein, PhD (1999)

Energy Medicine for Women
Donna Eden and David Feinstein, PhD (2008)

Energy Psychology Interactive - CD: Core Beliefs Table (2004)
David Feinstein, PhD

Energy Psychology Interactive - CD: Energy Medicine Topics (2004)
David Feinstein, PhD

Healing from Within: The Use of Hypnosis in Women's Health Care
Edited by Lynne M. Hornyak and Joseph P. Green (2000)
Chapter 11: Hypnosis in the Treatment of Eating Disorders by Marianne Barabasz

Invisible Roots
Dr. Barbara Stone, PhD (2008)

REBprotocol.net
Phillip Warren with Janet Nestor

T'ai Chi Ch'uan
Master T.T. Lang (1977)

The Association of Meridian and Energy Therapies
Forms of Psychological Reversals
http://theamt.com/search/?query=psychological+reversals&submit=Search

Autonomic Nervous System References

Adrenal Fatigue: The 21st Century Stress Syndrome
James L. Wilson, ND, DC, PhD (2011)

Autonomic Nervous System Health
Dr. Larry Wilson, MD
www.drwilson.com/articles/NERVOUS%SYSTEM.htm

Chronic Fatigue, Fibromyalgia & Lyme Disease, 2nd Edition
Burton Goldberg and Larry Trivieri, Jr. (2004)

Clinical Autonomic Disorders 3rd Edition
Phillip A. Low and Eduardo E. Benarroch (2008)

ClinicalPosters.com
Clinical Posters Staff:
http://clinicalposters.com/news/2011/0325-dysautonomia-mitochondria-pots.html

Dysautonomia (12 Stressors Behind the Total Stress Load Index)
CE Gant MD, PhD: http://cegant.com/Dysautonomia-12-Stressors.pdf

Living Well With Chronic Fatigue Syndrome and Fibromyalgia
Mary J. Shomon (2004)

MerckManuals.com http://www.merckmanuals.com/home/brain_spinal_cord_and_nerve_
disorders/autonomic_nervous_system_disorders/overview_of_the_autonomic_nervous_
system.html

The Autonomic Nervous System
John Newport Langley (1921)

Affirmation References

Association of Comprehensive Energy Psychology DCEP Training Manual
Psychological Reversals

Hospice
www.hospicenet.org/html/affirmations.html

The Positive Mindset Website
www.vitalaffirmations.com/index.phpUndert

Bmindful
http://bmindful.com/affirmations/forgiveness

Bmindful
http://bmindful.com/affirmations/esteem

Anxiety and Emotional Health References

Effects of mindfulness meditation training on anticipatory alpha modulation in primary somatosensory cortex: Kerr, Catherine E. Jones, Stephanie R., wan, Qian, Pritchett, Dominique L., Wexler, Anna, Villanueva, Joel J., Shaw, Jessica R., Lazar, Sara W., Kaptchuk, Ted J., Littenberg, Ronnie, Mamalaien, Matti S. More, Christopher L.: Brain Research Bulletin: April, 2011.

Laughter is the Best Medicine
Helpguide.org: http://www.helpguide.org/life/humor_laughter_health.htm

Healing With the Angels
Doreen Virtue, PhD (1999)

Living in Process
Ann Wilson Schaef (1999)
http://www.livinginprocess.com

Losing Pounds of Pain
Doreen Virtue, PhD (2002)

Love and Survival: The Scientific Basis for the Healing Power of Intimacy
Dr. Dean Ornish, MD (1998)

Meal by Meal: 365 Daily Meditations for Finding Balance through Mindful Eating
Donald Altman (2004)

Mindfulness Based Stress Reduction
http://www.umassmed.edu/cfm/stress/index.aspx

Pathways to Wholeness
Janet Gallagher Nestor (2010)

Relaxation and Stress Reduction Workbook
Martha Davis, PhD, Elizabeth Robbins Eshelman, MSW, Matthew McKay, PhD (2008)

SpiritLibrary.com
http://spiritlibrary.com/doreen-virtue/angel-numbers
Healing With the Angels/Doreen Virtue

Understanding Major Anxiety Disorders and Addiction, Co-occurring Disorders Series
Katie Evens (2003)

Graphics and Photographs

Brain Stem Diagram: p. 51: © Can Stock Photo Inc. / roxanabalint

Chakra Diagram: p. 52: Graphic by Mack Miller

Harmony hand positions: p. 30: Photos by Kirtan Coan

Heart Massage Graphic: p. 43: Courtesy of Dr. Barbara Stone, drawn by Jennifer Robinett

Janet Nestor's photograph: back cover: Jennifer Nestor-Cardwell, Sandy Springs, Georgia

REB posture Graphic: p. 43, 62: www.rebprotocol.net Graphic by Phillip Warren

Tapping Crown Center: p. 213: Kirtan Coan

Today

* * * * * * *

I choose to live in harmony.

With self,
With life,
With others,
With Mother Nature,
With Earth,
With Spirit,
With Creation.

Amen

~ *Janet Gallagher Nestor*